A LUTHERAN *looks at...*
BAPTISTS

Eric S. Hartzell

Northwestern Publishing House
Milwaukee, Wisconsin

Art Director: Karen Knutson
Designer: Pamela Dunn

All Scripture quotations, unless otherwise indicated, are taken from the HOLY BIBLE, NEW INTERNATIONAL VERSION®. NIV®. Copyright © 1973, 1978, 1984 by International Bible Society. Used by permission of Zondervan. All rights reserved.

All rights reserved. This publication may not be copied, photocopied, reproduced, translated, or converted to any electronic or machine-readable form in whole or in part, except for brief quotations, without prior written approval from the publisher.

LCCN: 2009924258
Northwestern Publishing House
1250 N. 113th St., Milwaukee, WI 53226-3284
www.nph.net
© 2010 by Northwestern Publishing House
Published 2010
Printed in the United States of America
ISBN 978-0-8100-2109-9

CONTENTS

	Introduction................................	iv
1	Baptist Beginnings	1
2	The Various Baptist Churches in the United States.........................	6
3	Baptist Creeds.............................	20
4	Baptist Teaching on Scripture	27
5	The Baptist Understanding of the Triune God..........................	31
6	Baptist Teaching on Conversion..............	34
7	Baptist Teaching on Baptism	40
8	Baptist Teaching on the Lord's Supper.........	49
9	Baptists on Marriage and Family	53
10	The Baptists' Life of Faith and Good Works	58
11	Baptist Church Organization	65
	Conclusion and Applications	70
	Addendum	79
	Endnotes.................................	127
	Bibliography	132

INTRODUCTION

When Jesus commissioned Christians in Matthew 28:20 to do his work and to spread his name, he told us to teach people to obey "everything I have commanded you."

This passage is the reason for this book. We want our teachings to agree with what Jesus taught. His Word is our only guide. So when we encounter teaching that runs counter to our teaching, we must go to the Word of God and find out what indeed is Jesus' teaching and what is not.

God also tells us, "Always be prepared to give an answer to everyone who asks you to give the reason for the hope that you have. But do this with gentleness and respect" (1 Peter 3:15). When we are called on to discuss Bible teachings with members of other churches, the Lord wants us to do this with gentleness and respect.

Gentleness and respect come when we are fair and precise in our understanding of what other churches believe. When Lutherans look at the Baptist church, they want to see it as it truly is and not as they imagine it to be. That is why most of the references to Baptist church teachings have come directly from statements of belief issued by the Baptist church.

Charles Ryrie, a professor at Dallas Seminary, has said:
Whenever you state the case of someone disagreeing with you, imagine that your opponent is sitting in the front row of the class. State his position in such a way that he would say, "Yes, that is what I believe." And then you can take issue with the position.[1]

The person who quoted Ryrie went on to say, "It is dishonest to characterize someone else's position in a way that person would disavow. Being precise and fair, even with differing viewpoints, also adds to our credibility."[2]

It would be impossible in the scope of a book like this to look at every belief held by the Baptists. Much of what Baptists believe are teachings Lutherans believe as well. When a Baptist leader says, for instance, "The Lord measures the gift by the love and sacrifice it involves,"[3] Lutherans agree wholeheartedly. But there are differences of belief between Baptists and Lutherans, and this book will deal with these important differences of belief.

We do not intend to be negative. We believe that Scripture must speak whenever differing beliefs are evaluated. We believe that when Scripture does speak, we must believe it and accept it, interpreting its words in the most natural sense. We believe that Scripture must interpret Scripture. As confessional Lutherans, we have expressed our agreement with those who formulated our doctrines and wrote them down in what we call *The Book of Concord*. What they did helps us to know what the Scripture truly says. We are convinced, however, that all our evaluations of Baptist and Lutheran teachings must begin and end with Scripture.

George Truett, at the Baptist World Congress in 1939, said:
> We profoundly rejoice in our spiritual union with all who love the Lord Jesus Christ in sincerity and truth. We cherish them as brothers in the saving grace of Christ, and heirs with us of life and immortality. We love their fellowship, and maintain that the spiritual union of all true believers in Christ is now, and will ever be, a blessed reality.[4]

We Lutherans believe the same thing! When other believers tell us that they believe that Jesus is their Savior, we rejoice. We know we will spend eternity with those people. We rejoice when we hear Baptists say:
> Baptists are a people who profess a living faith. This faith is rooted and grounded in Jesus Christ who is "The same yesterday, and today, and for ever." Therefore, the sole

authority for faith and practice among Baptists is Jesus Christ whose will is revealed in the Holy Scriptures.[5]

May this truly be so!

Lutherans can also very much appreciate that Baptists really know their Bibles. We could hope and wish that all Lutherans would have the same zeal to know and memorize Scripture as many Baptists have. Baptists sometimes carry dog-eared Bibles with them and know where to find the Bible passages they need. Surely the Lord who says, "You diligently study the Scriptures . . . that testify about me" (John 5:39) is glad when he sees this. In this regard Baptist believers can in many instances be an inspiration to Lutheran believers.

But there are differences among Christian churches, and there are differences between the Lutheran church and the Baptist church. Hence this book. We don't point to these differences happily. We wish it were different. But it isn't, and our churches are divided on a number of important teachings of the Bible. We as Lutherans don't find our identity in differing with other Christians. We find our identity in doing what Jesus tells us to do: ". . . teaching them to obey everything I have commanded you" (Matthew 28:20).

In this spirit the following 11 chapters present the major differences between the Lutheran church and the Baptist church. In studying these chapters, the reader will want to become even more convinced that what we teach as Lutherans is what Jesus has commanded his church to teach and profess.

1 BAPTIST BEGINNINGS

Some Baptists today are uncomfortable with being called Baptist. They say, "It isn't really important—or even good—to be identified as Baptist and to become a part of Baptist history." They would prefer to simply be called Christians who happen to be attending a church called Baptist. To some degree Lutherans would agree with this sentiment. Luther wasn't in favor of his followers being called Lutherans. Most confessional Lutherans today want to be identified as Christian first and Lutheran second. Surely the Christian part is the most important.

Yet the title "Lutheran" is also important. Lutherans want to know what their church teaches. Understanding its history helps them do this. To some degree where we've come from as a church affects who we are and how we express ourselves in matters of faith. This is also true for Christians in the Wisconsin Evangelical Lutheran Synod (WELS). The very name contains a reference to history. WELS Lutherans also identify who they are because so many other Lutheran bodies have not been true to historical Lutheranism and the name itself. So those who examine a church must also look at its history in order to understand how that church became what it is today.

Most churches will acknowledge that they started at some point in time. Most Baptists will acknowledge this to be true in their case also. But there are a few Baptists who claim the Baptist church goes all the way back to Adam! That claim seems pretty far-fetched even to most Baptists.

There is a larger group, however (which is still relatively small), that claims that the Baptist church goes back in one long, uninterrupted line to the time of Jesus and John the

Baptist. There is the so-called *JJJ Theory*, according to which the Baptist church goes back to Jesus, Jordan, and John the Baptist. It is, perhaps, natural that the church that calls itself Baptist would like to see the greatest of baptizers as its founder. Recall that the Roman Catholic Church claims that Matthew 16:18 supports the papacy and an unbroken line of succession to the present pope. Those who hold to the JJJ Theory claim that this passage also supports the Baptist church's continuing unbroken line of ordination up to the present day.[6] Those who believe this are called Baptist Successionists.

Some say that the Baptist church has existed *in perpetuity*. A group who call themselves Landmark Baptists think of their church in this way. Their belief is called Landmarkism. The "landmark" idea comes from two passages in Proverbs that talk about landmarks: "Do not move an ancient boundary stone set up by your forefathers" (Proverbs 22:28) and "Do not move an ancient boundary stone" (Proverbs 23:10). They believe that the Lord must keep his earthly church intact if he is to be trusted to keep our salvation intact. In their belief, of course, the true Christian church is the Baptist church, specifically, the church of the Landmark Baptists. J. R. Graves, an early proponent of Landmarkism, even said, "I deny that a man is a believer in the Bible who denies this."[7] The Landmark Baptists split from the Southern Baptist Convention in the late 19th and early 20th centuries. They claimed that the teachings of the Southern Baptist Convention had been degraded to the point that they no longer reflected the teaching of Christ's true church. They accused the Southern Baptist Convention of "moving the landmarks" of the true Baptist church.

There are also many who do not want the Baptist church to be called Protestant because they do not want to give people the impression that their church was ever connected to the Roman Catholic Church. (Protestantism refers to the movement within the Catholic Church to reform the teaching of the Catholic Church and cleanse it from error.)

However, history doesn't support the idea that the Baptist church was formed already in Jesus' day. In some respects, the Baptist church had its beginning in the Reformation. Those who first espoused ideas that were later to be taught by the Baptist church were called the Anabaptists. *Anabaptist* means "rebaptizer." It refers to the distinct teaching that Baptism in the Catholic Church was not valid because one needs to make a conscious and informed decision to believe in Jesus before one can be saved and baptized. The Anabaptists developed into the Mennonites, Hutterites, Amish, and Quakers.

The Anabaptists of Reformation times were what we would call Arminian in belief. (This will be discussed further in the section of the book that talks about the teachings and beliefs of the Baptist church.) Arminianism contained a faulty belief about the powers of sinful man. Arminianism believed that people could accept God by their own decision and choice. The Baptist religion did not teach Arminianism at first but held to a more Calvinistic doctrine. Yet their insistence on believer's baptism put them in the Arminian Anabaptist camp from the start. Later on, as we will see, most Baptists gave up Calvinism in favor of Arminianism.

In 1530, Lutherans were already making statements against Anabaptist beliefs. Much of what they said against this group can also be said against the Baptists. The Augsburg Confession makes many references to Anabaptist beliefs. Fifty years after the Augsburg Confession, the Formula of Concord also spoke against the Anabaptist beliefs. Both confessions speak against what would become Baptist belief in the matters of conversion, the human nature and will, the life of love a Christian leads, and its proper place in the order of salvation. They also speak against Anabaptist beliefs about the Lord's Supper and Baptism, especially in regard to infant Baptism.

Consider the following statements from Article 12 of the Epitome to the Formula of Concord ("Errors Which Cannot be Tolerated in the Church"). These statements speak about the matter of infant Baptism, which the Anabaptists rejected. The Lutheran Confessions reject these ideas:

> That in the sight of God unbaptized children are not sinners but are righteous and innocent, and that as long as they have not achieved the use of reason they will be saved in this innocence without Baptism (which according to this view they do not need). They [the Anabaptists] thus reject the entire doctrine of original sin and everything that pertains to it.
>
> That children are not to be baptized until they have achieved the use of reason and can confess their faith personally.
>
> That without and prior to Baptism the children of Christian parents are holy and the children of God by virtue of their birth from Christian and pious parents. For this reason, too, the Anabaptists neither think highly of infant Baptism nor encourage it, in spite of the expressed word of God's promise which extends only to those who keep his covenant and do not despise it.[8]

These statements on Baptism define some of the major differences that exist between the Lutheran and Baptist churches.

So where and when did the Baptist church come into being?

There are two ideas as to where the present-day Baptist church actually came from, not counting the successionist idea discussed previously. Some believe it came directly from the Anabaptists as they spread from Switzerland to other countries because of persecution. Others believe that the Baptist church came from the English Separatist Movement of the 16th century, which wanted to rid the English church of all vestiges of Roman Catholicism. They were dissatisfied with the mere outward break that took place, because many of the Catholic practices and beliefs were retained by the new Church of England. You may be familiar with the Puritans. They wanted to stay with the Church of England but wanted to "purify" it of its errors. The Baptists, however, said that the answer lay in complete separation. The best answer is that both were true. The Anabaptist influence on the Puritans and Separatists in England cannot be disputed.

The earliest Baptist church can be traced back to 1609 in Amsterdam, with John Smyth as pastor. Smyth had become a Puritan about 15 years earlier, but he and his group separated from the Church of England. Persecution followed, and Smyth and his followers fled from England to Holland. His followers rebaptized themselves and declared Christ as their Savior. This adult Baptism became the seminal event in the early Baptist church and led to its being given the name Baptist. They maintained that infant Baptism was meaningless because babies couldn't fulfill the requirement of Baptism, namely, coming to faith in Christ and performing an outward act of obedience as a sign of one's commitment to Christ.

It is unknown when the first Baptist church in America was founded. The honor seems to be split between two churches. Both Roger Williams and his colleague in working for religious freedom, Dr. John Clarke, have received credit. Williams established a Baptist church in Providence, Rhode Island, and Clarke began a Baptist church in Newport, Rhode Island.

THE VARIOUS BAPTIST CHURCHES
in the United States

If we look at the following chart of the ten largest churches in the United States, we see that Baptists make up a large percentage of the Christian population of our country:

The Roman Catholic Church: 66.4 million
The Southern Baptist Convention: 16.24 million
The United Methodist Church: 8.25 million
The Church of God in Christ: 5.49 million
The Church of Jesus Christ of Latter-day Saints: 5.41 million
The Evangelical Lutheran Church in America: 5.03 million
The National Baptist Convention USA, Inc.: 5 million
The National Baptist Convention of America, Inc.: 3.5 million
Presbyterian Church (USA): 3.4 million
Assemblies of God: 2.68 million[9]

The three largest Baptist groups together include 24.74 million people! When we look at the Baptist church in its entirety, we're looking at a large assortment of different Baptist churches with different names and different teachings. Yet they all carry the name Baptist. They think of themselves as Baptists. It is not easy to determine exactly how one group differs from another. Even Baptists acknowledge this fact when in their official statements they refer to the "extreme diversity of the Baptist Church in America."[10] We will study this in the next chapter when we look at both the confessional diversity among the Baptists and also what they agree on. We will see that because Baptists shy away from confessional standards, it is easy for differences to develop.

To understand the Baptists, we must have some idea of where Baptist teachings came from. Lutherans follow the teachings of Martin Luther. (Some Lutheran churches today stray far from Luther's teachings while others stay close to them.) Besides Martin Luther, John Calvin and Jacob Arminius were important teachers in the Protestant Movement, whose teachings have been accepted by any number of contemporary Christian denominations. Denominations in the Calvinist tradition are Presbyterian, Dutch and German Reformed, Episcopalian, Baptist, and Congregationalist. Those in the Arminian tradition are Methodist, Holiness groups like the Nazarenes and the Salvation Army, and Pentecostal groups like the Assemblies of God.

In some cases, however, there is not a clear-cut distinction because some denominations, such as Baptist and Episcopalian, have churches in both traditions. On its Web page, Word of His Grace Ministries, a Calvanist group, says "Today, Arminianism pervades the teaching of most Protestant (including Baptist) churches."[11]

Baptists themselves recognize the influence of both Arminius and Calvin on their churches. Most people will conclude that Arminianism predominates in the Baptist church today. But this forces a Reformed Baptist pastor to say the following:

> In this "Reformed" tradition are the great names of Church history. John Calvin, John Knox, John Bunyan, John Newton, Matthew Henry, George Whitefield, Jonathan Edwards, Adoniram Judson, William Carey, C. H. Spurgeon, A. W. Pink, and a host of others held tenaciously to the Reformed Faith (Calvinistic beliefs). We must underscore, however, that we hold to these truths not because Calvin and these other great men of church history held to them, but because Jesus and the apostles so clearly taught them.

Out of this theological understanding came great Reformed confessions and creeds—the Synod of Dort, The Westminister Confession of Faith, The Heildberg Confession and Catechism. Our own Confession of Faith is deeply rooted in these historic Reformed Documents (in most places it is a word for word copy), which is why, historically and theologically, we lay hold of the title Reformed.[12]

Yet many Baptist churches do, in fact, lean toward the Arminian tradition and follow to some extent the teachings of Jacob Arminius. Arminianism can be summarized as follows:
- Man is sick in sin but not dead in sin. He can do something toward his salvation.
- God chooses who will be saved based on his foreknowledge, if only they will exercise their free will to believe.
- Jesus' atoning death was for all people . . . even those who would reject it.
- When God offers grace to a person, he can reject it.
- It is possible to choose to stop believing in Jesus.[13]

By contrast, Calvin and his followers believe:
- Man is dead in sin and can do nothing toward his salvation. (Total Depravity)
- God chooses who will be saved purely because he is gracious and not because of what he sees in the person. (Unconditional Election)[14]
- Jesus' atoning death was only for the believers. (Limited Atonement)
- When God offers grace to whom he offers it, that person cannot reject it. (Irresistable Grace)
- It is impossible to choose to give up one's faith once a person believes. (Perseverance of the Saints)

In comparison, we might express Lutheran beliefs like this:
- By nature all people are completely dead in sin.
- Our salvation is entirely a work of God's grace.

- There is unlimited atonement, since Christ's work covers the sins of all people.
- We have the power to resist the Spirit's work in our hearts.
- Christians have the ability to lose their faith.

Lutherans agree with Calvinists on the first two and with Arminians on the last three.

At the Synod of Dort (1618–1619), Dutch theologians responded to the teachings of Arminius and came up with the five points of Calvinism. Those who signed the (Baptist) 1689 London Confession of Faith were solidly Reformed. They wrote:

> We the MINISTERS, and MESSENGERS of, and concerned for upwards of, one hundred BAPTIZED CHURCHES, in England and Wales (denying Arminianism), being met together in London, from the third of the seventh month to the eleventh of the same, 1689, to consider of some things that might be for the glory of God, and the good of these congregations, have thought meet (for the satisfaction of all other Christians that differ from us in the point of Baptism) to recommend to their perusal the confession of our faith, which confession we own, as containing the doctrine of our faith and practice, and do desire that the members of our churches respectively do furnish themselves therewith.[15]

Between the writing of the London Confession of Faith and today, Baptists have injected a fair amount of Arminianism into their theology. Understanding the tension between Arminian and Calvinistic theology helps us understand the differences that exist among present-day Baptist churches.

The Southern Baptist Convention

The Southern Baptist Convention (SBC) is the largest of the Baptist church organizations. Since its organization in 1845 in Augusta, Georgia, the Southern Baptist Convention has grown to more than 16 million members who worship in more than

42,000 churches in the United States. Southern Baptists sponsor about five thousand home missionaries serving the United States, Canada, Guam, and the Caribbean, as well as more than five thousand foreign missionaries in 153 nations of the world. The Southern Baptist Convention is the second largest religious body in the United States. It has more churches (over 37,000) in the United States than any other religious body—even more than the Roman Catholic Church.[16]

This convention split with the northern Baptists prior to the Civil War over the question of slavery. At that time the SBC had African-American members. After the Civil War that element dropped out and the SBC became a "white" church.

The title "Southern Baptist Convention" refers to both the denomination and its annual meeting. Working through 1,200 local associations and 41 state conventions and fellowships, Southern Baptists share a common bond of basic biblical beliefs and a stated commitment to proclaim the gospel of Jesus Christ to the entire world.

According to the Web site from which much of the above is taken, one becomes a Southern Baptist by uniting with a Southern Baptist church that is in friendly cooperation with the general Southern Baptist enterprise of reaching the world for Christ. We read that typically church membership is a matter of accepting Jesus as your Savior and Lord (Arminian belief) and experiencing believer's baptism by immersion. The fact that Jesus died for our sins, was buried, and then rose from the grave is considered foundational to being considered a Southern Baptist.[17]

The American Baptist Church

American Baptists say that they are

> a Christ-centered, biblically grounded, ethnically diverse people called to radical personal discipleship in Christ Jesus. Our commitment to Jesus propels us to nurture authentic relationships with one another; build healthy churches; transform our communities, our nations and our world; engage every member in hands-on ministry;

and speak the prophetic word in love. As a people of prayer, purpose, and passion, we are in the forefront of creating a community of faith where people of every race, nationality and culture gather united in worship, service and work.[18]

The General Secretary welcomes viewers to the official Web site with the following:

It is my great joy to welcome you to the Web site of the American Baptist Churches USA. From Adoniram Judson to Dr. Martin Luther King Jr., from Helen Barrett Montgomery to Walter Rauschenbusch, American Baptists are a denomination of rich history and diversity.[19]

The internal 1972 Study Commission on Denominational Structures stressed the importance of insuring proportional representation of women, men, African-Americans, Hispanics, Asians, Caucasians, and Indians on the American Baptist General Board, national program boards, and committees. Policies and goals were established to create inclusive national staffs with respect to gender and race.

Listen to this self-critique of the American Baptists:

The diversity of American Baptists brings many gifts to our denominational family. We have made much progress but have not yet achieved the goal of true inclusiveness. The diversity we experience as a national body is most often absent in our local churches. We do not create sufficient opportunities to listen to one another, to grow in understanding, to share in one another's lives. To a large extent, our churches still are largely separated racially and ethnically, sometimes due to community patterns. While more and more churches are seeking to work together across racial and cultural lines, we must continue to find new ways to bridge our separations.[20]

The American Baptists realize how theologically diverse the Baptist church is. They say:

Theological diversity has been prevalent in our history and nature as Baptists. The adjectives with which we Baptists have through the years identified ourselves have often indicated our varied theological understandings. (i.e., General, Particular, Six-Principle, Seventh Day, Free will, Regular, Separate, Landmark, Primitive and Missionary.) While theological diversity has often separated Baptists from one another, American Baptists have sought an inclusive fellowship based on a common allegiance to Jesus Christ as Savior and Lord.[21]

The American Baptist church has struggled with the homosexual issue. Rev. Daniel Weiss, general secretary of the American Baptist Church U.S.A., said in an interview that the homosexual issue is "not at the central core of the Christian faith." He said: "When you stop to think of the millions of people in the world who have things done to them, who are hungry or who are exploited by other people, why would you get all bent out of shape and worry about people who are doing what they want with each other?"[22] Yet a resolution passed by the church on the homosexual issue says, "We affirm that the practice of homosexuality is incompatible with Christian teaching."[23] It's interesting to note that the vote included 110 Yes votes, 64 No votes, and 5 abstentions.[24]

General Association of Regular Baptist Churches

Twenty-two Baptist churches of the American Baptist Convention left that group in May of 1932 to found a new group. They were protesting modernist tendencies and teachings in the American Convention and the denial of the historic Baptist principle of the independence and autonomy of the local congregation.

Among its beliefs, the General Association of Regular Baptist Churches believes in two biblical ordinances: baptism by immersion and the Lord's Supper. The teachings of the millennium and the rapture are endorsed, along with the belief that the nation of Israel will be restored and saved at the second coming of Christ.[25]

General Baptists

The movement of churches today called General Baptists began in America in 1823 when founder Benoni Stinson organized the Liberty Church (now Howell General Baptist Church) in southern Indiana. In 1870 the General Association of General Baptists was organized, bringing together General Baptist local associations of churches to engage in cooperative efforts.

General Baptists do not believe in the perseverance of the saints. (In this they accept the Arminian belief.) "We believe that those who abide in Christ have the assurance of salvation. However, we believe that the Christian retains his freedom of choice; therefore, it is possible for him to turn away from God and be finally lost."[26] In this they part company with many Baptists who believe in the perseverance of the saints. In many ways General Baptists are similar to the Free Will Baptists and are more Arminian in nature.

The National Baptist Convention USA

The National Baptist Convention USA, Inc., was founded in 1886. It is the nation's oldest and largest African-American religious convention, with an estimated membership of 7.5 million.

It lists among its priorities:

> . . . to promote home and foreign mission efforts, to encourage and support Christian education, to publish and distribute Sunday School and other Christian literature, music, and other works of art and religious expression; and to engage in any other endeavors deemed fitting and proper in order to advance the cause of Jesus Christ throughout the world.[27]

The National Baptist Convention of America

The National Baptist Convention of America, Inc., is different from the National Baptist Convention USA. It is an amalgamation of three Baptist groups: the Foreign Mission Baptist Convention of the United States (1880), the American National Baptist Convention (1886), and the Baptist National Educational Convention (1893). These bodies originally met in the Friendship Baptist Church (Atlanta, Georgia) in 1895 to unify their mission work (domestic and foreign), foster the cause of education, and promote the publication and circulation of religious literature. The result of this meeting was the emergence of the new organization under the name National Baptist Convention of America.[28]

The Reformed Baptist Church

The Association of Reformed Baptist Churches of America was founded on March 11, 1997. On that day the first General Assembly met to establish a charter membership of 24 churches from 14 states. Since then it has grown to 34 churches and continues to expand.[29] This church organization (ARBCA) "longs to have" its own seminary and publishing house.

The word *reformed* used in the title of this church body expresses a commitment to the biblical doctrines that are best summarized in the London Baptist Confession of 1689.[30] It is the stated desire of this group to constantly reform its faith and practice according to the standard of the Word of God.[31]

If the very number of different Baptist church bodies makes a Lutheran's head swim, consider how a Reformed Baptist pastor's head swims as he contemplates the differences within the Reformed Baptist Church.

There exists an ever widening gulf between churches that call themselves Reformed Baptists. The term has not been copyrighted and thus there exists no definitive statement regarding who can lay claim to the title. No two Reformed Baptist churches walk in lock step. There are churches who call themselves "Reformed Baptists" and all that they mean by that is that they hold to the so-called five points of Calvinism and they immerse believers. There are "Reformed Baptists" who believe in pastoral oversight as an integral part of the life of the church and there are other "Reformed Baptists" who say that pastoral oversight is an abuse of power. There are "Reformed Baptists" who hold to the *Second London Baptist Confession of Faith of 1689* and there are those who hold to but a few of the articles. While most Reformed Baptists hold to a biblical and puritan view of the Lord's Day Sabbath, there are some "Reformed Baptists" who reject the doctrine as legalistic. You will furthermore find Reformed Baptists churches who differ in regard to their understanding of the exact application of the regulative principle of worship (the conviction that the Bible alone dictates the worship of the church). You will find differences in who is invited to the Lord's table, differences in Bible translations, hymnals, and the structure of prayer meetings. The list could go on and on.[32]

Primitive Baptists

The name Primitive Baptist became popular in the early 1800s when the term *primitive* conveyed the idea of originality rather than backwardness. Accordingly, Primitive Baptists claim to maintain the doctrines and practices of the original Baptists, who also claimed to be the true New Testament church. *Primitive* is also used to convey the idea of simplicity. This well describes the Primitive Baptists, whose church services consist of nothing more than preaching, praying, and singing. This group keeps the name Primitive because the very word provokes interest and questions regarding what they are about. (This is their hope anyway.)

Some other names given to Primitive Baptists are Old School, Regular, Anti-mission, and Hard Shell.

When asked what the difference is between them and other Baptists, Primitive Baptists answer that the question is almost impossible to answer because of the extreme diversity of modern Baptists. The official statement of the Primitive Baptists goes on to say:

> Consequently, we assume that the reader has his or her own concept of what a Baptist is, and we leave it to the

reader to make their own judgment as to how this question should be answered. People wondering about Primitive Baptist identity are asked to examine the Articles of Faith and the Abstract to the Doctrine of Salvation. The Black Rock Address of 1832 will acquaint the inquisitive with the circumstances which led to the division between Primitive and other Baptists.[33]

Primitive Baptists view Scripture as the divinely inspired Word of God and as the sole rule of faith and practice for the church. Primitive Baptists also believe that Scripture has been divinely preserved over the ages and that the 1611 King James Version is the superior English translation of Scripture.[34]

Free Will Baptists

If these different Baptist church groups get confusing, listen to what the Free Will Baptists say on their Web site, "This site is not affiliated with the National Association of Free Will Baptists, Inc."

The Free Will Baptists believe in free will! (Remember again that this is one of the tenets of Arminianism.) Free Will Baptists practice baptism by immersion. They list three ordinances of the gospel as the Lord's Supper, Baptism, and the Washing of the Saints' Feet. The first day of the week is to be reserved for sacred activities and for refraining from secular labor.

Seventh Day Baptist General Conference

These Baptists call themselves evangelical Baptists and hold to keeping the Sabbath Day. This group goes back to 1671 in Newport, Rhode Island. They characterize themselves as a "Christ-centered, Bible believing people with traditional family values."[35] They presently have churches in North America and in more than 20 countries.

Separate Baptists in Christ

The Separate Baptists describe their church as follows:

> We believe that Baptism, the Lord's Supper and feet washing are ordained of Christ appointed in the Church

and none, but true believers, are proper subjects, and that immersion is the Gospel mode of baptism.

We believe in the sanctity of the first day of the week, or Lord's Day, and it should be spent in public or private worship, and we abstain from worldly concerns, except in case of necessity or mercy. [The Lord's Day observance here is different from the Sabbath observance of the Seventh Day Baptists discussed previously.]

We believe that, at Christ's coming in the clouds of Heaven, all Christians will be gathered with Him in the clouds and that time shall be no more, thus leaving no time for a literal one thousand year reign."[36]

United Baptists

United Baptists are unaffiliated local associations of churches that have remained separate and distinct from any national organization. The *Churches and Church Membership in the United States* 1990 survey found more than 54,000 members in 436 churches and 24 associations. Approximately 27 such associations exist in the United States, and they fall roughly into three groups: (1) United Baptist (General) congregations are somewhat Arminian, open Communion bodies. They fellowship with other bodies that are moderately Calvinistic and practice closed Communion. (2) United Baptist (Landmark) congregations are moderately Calvinistic, practice closed Communion, and once cooperated loosely with the Southern Baptist Convention. (3) United Baptist (Regular) congregations are primitivistic and practice closed Communion. The largest concentration of these churches is in Kentucky.

Many United Baptists remain unaffiliated and differ from one another in their views on the atonement, on the teaching that believers cannot fall from faith, and on prerequisites for Communion fellowship. They are fairly consistent in avoiding general unions and conventions, observe the ordinance of feet washing, and prefer an itinerant unsalaried ministry. A majority of their churches tend to primitivism and reject a trained ministry, Sunday schools, and even instrumental music. Most prefer baptizing with natural water. Associations promote fellowship by "corresponding" with (sending representatives to) other associations that they deem to be of "like faith and order."[37]

Two-Seed-in-the-Spirit Predestinarian Baptists

This is a small group of Baptists most closely related in teaching to the Primitive Baptists, although they do not consider themselves Primitive Baptists. They believe that every child at birth has either a seed of good implanted or a seed of evil. (This belief can be traced back to Arminianism discussed previously.)

In 2003 there appeared to be four Two-Seed-in-the-Spirit Predestinarian Baptist churches (two in Texas, and one each in Indiana and Tennessee) with approximately 80 members. Two of the churches participate together in the Trinity River Association, and two are independent.[38]

General Six-Principle Baptists

The official statement for the General Six-Principle Baptists shows their Arminian leanings:

> We are called "General" because the majority of those associated with our denomination, past and present, adhere to the atonement of Christ as being "general" in nature, or for all people as opposed to being just for the elect, or a few.[39]

This group believes in "believer's baptism" as the biblical directive as opposed to infant Baptism. According to their name, they also claim to follow the six principles of Hebrews 6:1,2. They lay special emphasis on the fourth of these "principles," which is the laying on of hands. They believe that the rest of the Baptists, although they may at times lay on hands, have missed this point and do not practice the laying on of hands correctly in the sense of Hebrews 6:1,2.

This may not be a complete list, but it will give the reader a good idea of the diversity of Baptist groups.

3 BAPTIST CREEDS

The Lutheran church expects its pastors and members to abide by the Lutheran Confessions. The next time you attend the ordination of a Lutheran pastor, pay attention to the fact that he is asked to promise to abide by *The Book of Concord*. *The Book of Concord* contains the creeds and confessions of the Lutheran church. Every pastor in a confessional Lutheran church studied those teachings in depth at the seminary when he prepared to become a pastor.

The contents of *The Book of Concord* are the three chief creeds of Christendom (the Apostles' Creed, the Nicene Creed, and the Athanasian Creed), the Augsburg Confession, the Apology of the Augsburg Confession, the Smalcald Articles and the Treatise on the Power and Primacy of the Pope, the Small Catechism, the Large Catechism, and the Formula of Concord. In the Lutheran church, the confessions are documents whose authority is ruled or guided by an authority that is above them and that supercedes them. The authority that governs them is the authority of God's Word, the Holy Scriptures. This authority always remains over the confessions.

Yet Lutherans hold that their confessions are a correct exposition of God's Word, and so to them, the confessions are also authoritative. Confessional Lutherans abide by their confessions not *to the extent* that they agree with Scripture but *because* they agree with Scripture. This implies, of course, knowing what the confessions teach and having compared them with Scripture.[40]

The Baptist church is not a confessional church in the sense described above. In fact, it prides itself in not being a confessional or creedal church. Herschel H. Hobbs, who amplified

"The Baptist Faith and Message" statement into something of a creed, makes this disclaimer in his introduction:

> Baptists are an amazing people. They have no creed, yet they enjoy a remarkable unity. Scattered throughout the earth, having different ethnic backgrounds, living under varied types of government, and faced with problems inherent in different social environments, they share a unity in diversity. This unity is a living faith and an abiding message.
>
> It would be impossible for any one person to write an official statement of the Baptist faith and message. The writer of this book is a Southern Baptist. However, in no sense is this work a binding statement of faith and message for Southern Baptists. It is one Baptist's effort to interpret a statement which Southern Baptist messengers in assembled session voted as comprising a treatment of those basic elements of faith generally agreed upon by Southern Baptists. In large measure it is a statement in agreement with the faith and message of Baptists everywhere.[41]

Hobbs sums it up by saying, "It is sufficient to say that one's position as to details has never been a test of orthodoxy among Baptists."[42]

Two things are obvious from these statements of belief: Baptists don't make unified creedal statements and Baptists don't consider any such creedal statements to be binding on fellow Baptists. In a way, we could say that the Baptist creed is to have no creeds.

The Southern Baptist Convention in 1962 said in convention that the sole authority of faith and practice among Baptists is the Scriptures of the Old and New Testaments. Confessions are only guides in interpretation and have no authority over the conscience. That same convention said:

> Throughout their history Baptist bodies, both large and small, have issued statements of faith which comprise a consensus of their beliefs. Such statements have never

been regarded as complete, infallible statements of faith, nor as official creeds carrying mandatory authority. Thus this generation of Southern Baptists is in historic succession of intent and purpose as it endeavors to state for its time and theological climate those articles of the Christian faith which are most surely held among us.[43]

An example of "issued statements of faith" would be *The 1689 Confession of Faith*. Consider the topics discussed in that document in the context of the necessity of a statement of faith:

Of the Holy Scriptures
Of God and the Holy Trinity
Of God's Decree
Of Creation
Of Divine Providence
Of the Fall of Man, of Sin,
   and of the Punishment Thereof
Of God's Covenant
Of Christ the Mediator
Of Free Will
Of Effectual Calling
Of Justification
Of Adoption
Of Sanctification
Of Saving Faith
Of Repentance Unto Life and Salvation
Of Good Works
Of the Perseverance of the Saints
Of the Assurance of Grace and Salvation
Of the Law of God
Of the Gospel and the Extent of Grace thereof
Of Christian Liberty and Liberty of Conscience
Of Religious Worship and the Sabbath Day
Of Lawful Oaths and Vows
Of the Civil Magistrate

Of Marriage
Of the Church
Of the Communion of Saints
Of Baptism and the Lord's Supper
Of Baptism
Of the Lord's Supper
Of the State of Man After Death,
   and of the Resurrection of the Dead
Of the Last Judgment

Even Baptists have to admit that it isn't easy to live without creeds and confessions as Hobbs described. The Preamble to "The Baptist Faith and Message" of the Southern Baptist Convention says:

> Baptists are a people of deep beliefs and cherished doctrines. Throughout our history we have been a confessional people, adopting statements of faith as a witness to our beliefs and a pledge of our faithfulness to the doctrines revealed in Holy Scripture.
>
> Our confessions of faith are rooted in historical precedent, as the church in every age has been called upon to define and defend its beliefs. Each generation of Christians bears the responsibility of guarding the treasury of truth that has been entrusted to us (2 Timothy 1:14). Facing a new century, Southern Baptists must meet the demands and duties of the present hour.[44]

Note that the Southern Baptist Church calls itself "confessional."

Some Baptists question the stand of their own church on creeds and confessions. In an article appearing in the Baptist Press, one author writes:

> While no Baptist would want to put any confession on the same level with Scripture or confuse doctrinal statements about Jesus with a dynamic trust in Jesus, to say that the confession has no authority is certainly an overstatement and a wrongly informed understanding of our Baptist heritage. The confession is a secondary source of authority,

not a primary one like Holy Scripture. Nevertheless, confessions have historically been understood to have a normative place in the life of believers. . . . I am saying that a commitment to biblical inerrancy alone is insufficient. That is not enough to guarantee orthodoxy. There are Jehovah's Witnesses and other cults who claim belief in inerrancy. I am making a plea for the importance of confessional statements.[45]

In this statement, the writer actually agrees with the Lutheran understanding of the role of confessions.

Russell D. Moore, dean of the Theology School of Southern Baptist Theological Seminary, writes:

Maybe the recitation of the Apostles' Creed will put away all this nonsense about "no creed but the Bible." Maybe it will refocus the BWA leadership on what Baptists have always known—there is no cooperation without a common confessional conviction. And maybe one day the BWA will move away from the ambiguity of a "creedless" bureaucracy toward a defined orthodox Baptist witness in the world.[46]

The Southern Baptist Convention in its bylaws shows that it really does require confessional statements of its members. Consider the requirements in Bylaw 15, Committee on Nominations:

The Committee on Nominations traditionally sets the parameters for what constitutes a qualified person. Among others, these include 1) individuals who embrace the Baptist Faith & Message as the representative confession of faith among Southern Baptists, and 2) individuals whose churches have regularly given a substantial percentage of the undesignated receipts through the Cooperative Program.[47]

In spite of these statements, however, Baptists pride themselves in not having a formal confession of faith. It is easy to see that if there are no creeds and confessional statements by which church members can test whether pastors and people are interpreting and applying Scripture properly, that there will be great diversity in doctrine and practice. Some have even said that there is no greater diversity of teaching in any other Christian church than in the Baptist church.[48]

A recent example from the Southern Baptist churches of Georgia shows what happens when a church does not have binding creeds and confessions. The following transpired when Katrina Brooks became pastor of North Broad Baptist Church in Rome, Georgia.

Soon after becoming the only female senior pastor of an existing Southern Baptist church in Georgia, Brooks quickly learned that she wasn't welcome by everyone in the community. Two weeks after arriving in Rome, several clergy called meetings of the Floyd County Baptist Association to discuss the issue of female pastors.

The association, which had not yet adopted the 2000 "Baptist Faith and Message," suddenly was faced with a motion to vote on it—a move that Katrina and Tony Brooks believe was directed at them, although clergy in support of the statement insist it was simply a matter of aligning the local group with the regional and state conventions.

"If we adopt the Faith and Message statement, which I hope we do, it is essentially a statement made by the churches of Floyd County that this is what we believe. It is not meant to force out any church," said the Rev. Tony Cargle of New Antioch Baptist Church in Rome.

In April, the association's executive committee voted 82-22 to recommend that the full body adopt the statement at its annual meeting, scheduled for Monday.

Ratification would mean the Rome church could no longer be affiliated with the local association, and therefore could not be a member of the state convention.

However, it can still be a member of the SBC, a spokesman for the national body said.

If the association adopts the statement, it is "basically drawing a line in the sand for any church that does not affirm this message in its entirety," Katrina Brooks said.

"About a dozen churches in Georgia that opposed the 2000 Baptist Faith & Message have joined a rival organization called the Cooperative Baptist Fellowship," said Frank Broome, a spokesman for the group. Formed by moderates, the fellowship welcomes female pastors. (As of December 1997, there were 1,225 ordained women in the Southern Baptist Convention.)[49]

"The main issue with me is the question over whether our association has the power to dictate to the churches what they can do with their pastor situation or any other situation," said the Rev. Steve Skates of Hill Crest Baptist Church in Rome, which is 66 miles from Atlanta in northwest Georgia. But convention spokesman John Revell said the SBC always has remained true to its conservative interpretation of the Bible, and the statement simply articulates that. "That is what the Southern Baptist (Convention) has been from the start and continues to be," said Revell, emphasizing that the statement is "not a creed to which churches must adhere."[50]

When Lutherans look at a situation like this, they can be thankful to belong to a confessional and creedal church. Being confessional doesn't remove all of a church's problems. But it does give an agreed upon reference of correct Bible interpretation to all the congregations in the church, who agree to live by the standards of doctrine and practice agreed to by the church body they willingly joined. It also constantly points back to Scripture and to the correct understanding of it.

4 BAPTIST TEACHING *on Scripture*

When we study the teachings of another church body, we must understand how that church approaches the basis and rule of faith, namely, the Scriptures. How do the Lutheran and Baptist churches use God's Word as they defend and detail their teachings?

Both the Baptist church and the Lutheran church believe in the verbal inspiration of the Bible. Verbal inspiration says that in the original Greek and Hebrew manuscripts of Scripture, God was responsible for every single word. Every word that earthly writers wrote was God's Word. God "breathed into" them every word! "*All* Scripture is God-breathed and is useful for teaching, rebuking, correcting and training in righteousness, so that the man of God may be thoroughly equipped for every good work" (2 Timothy 3:16,17). In this both Baptists and Lutherans agree. They also agree that "prophecy never had its origin in the will of man, but men spoke from God as they were carried along by the Holy Spirit" (2 Peter 1:21).

Lutherans rejoice when they hear Baptists say, "We want to do what we do because we see it in our Bibles. 'To the law and to the testimony' must be upon our banner!"[51] But even though we rejoice and agree with this statement, there is still a difference between confessional Lutherans and Baptists. How do they understand and read the inspired words of God? What is their approach to what the words are actually saying to us?

Lutherans agree with one Reformed Baptist pastor who said:

> Therefore, as Reformed Baptists, but more particularly as serious biblically minded Christians, we reject the trends of our day toward shallow teaching, canceled preaching services, the giving of services of worship over to testimonies, movies, drama, dance, or singing. The Word of God is to be central in the worship of God. Paul warned of the day that would come when professed churchman would no longer tolerate sound doctrine. He stated that according to their own desires they would heap up for themselves teachers who would tickle their itching ears. The apostolic command thundered forth to Timothy in the midst of such mindless drivel, "Preach the Word!" (2 Tim. 4:1ff).[52]

Lutherans believe that the Word must remain central to a Christian's life and worship. The pillar of Martin Luther's life and theology was Scripture. One of his greatest accomplishments was his translation of the Bible into German. The Bible—Scripture—is one of the three *solas* upon which the Lutheran church was founded: by Scripture alone, by grace alone, by faith alone. Martin Luther constantly talked about our need to set reason aside when we approach Scripture. He believed our human reason can be an impediment to faith because reason insists on figuring everything out and understanding everything before it can believe. Reason, he taught, must be used to understand what Scripture says, but once it has found that out, reason must give way to faith.

The followers of Martin Luther believe there remain things about God's revelation that don't and can't fit into the narrow confines of our minds and our thinking processes. The teaching of the Lord's Supper is an example of a teaching that runs counter to reason. How can the body and blood of Jesus really be present in the Lord's Supper when we confess with the Christian church that Jesus with his resurrected body is now sitting at God's right hand? Reason would say this can't be true, that Jesus' body can only be locally present in one place at one time. Reason deduces that these words are spoken symbolically or figuratively. But if reason is set aside, as the Lutheran church believes it must be in cases like this, and if Scripture is taken at face value, the result is the belief that the body and blood are truly present with the bread and wine and that the same body of Jesus is truly present at God's right hand too. Jesus simply said, "Take and eat; this is my body. . . . This is my blood" (Matthew 26:26,28). Lutherans hold to these words and say this must be true.

There are statements that defy reason and logic. We can't always "get it" intellectually. But faith does not depend on getting it but on believing it. And that is possible by the working of God's Holy Spirit. When Lutherans come to this Word of God, which transcends human understanding, they come in the spirit of Martin Luther, who believed the following:

The Bible is not a book that was produced by reason and by the wisdom of men. The knowledge of lawyers and poets comes from reason and may, in turn, be understood and grasped by reason. But what Moses and the prophets teach does not stem from reason and the wisdom of men. Therefore he who presumes to comprehend Moses and the prophets with his reason and to measure agreement with reason will get away from the Bible entirely. From the very beginning all heretics owed their rise to the notion that what they had read in Scripture they were at liberty to explain according to the teachings of reason.[53]

So when Lutherans approach the Bible, they say to themselves, "I am going to believe this even though I can't understand everything. I'm going to believe this even though it doesn't make complete sense to me. I am not going to try to explain away the difficulties but will simply say, 'If that is what the words clearly say, I am going to believe it and accept it.'"

John Calvin believed that the Lord said nothing that is at variance with reason. To quote him, "Reason and faith are not opposed to each other. Hence we maintain that we must not admit anything, even in religious matters, which is contrary to right reason."[54]

This difference causes wide divergences between the Lutheran church and the Baptist church. This is the reason why the Lutheran church and the Baptist church can read the same Scripture and believe that it is God's Word—every word of it—and still come away with so many differences in major teachings. The Baptist church takes the "reasonable" approach. Luther, in opposition to this mind-set, maintained that reason has to be taken captive to the words of God and that Scripture is to be simply believed in the clearest and most easily understood way.

Understanding the different approach to Scripture is basic to understanding the other differences between the Baptist church and the Lutheran church. The belief we hold regarding how we read the inspired words of Scripture affects how we teach and practice it. This will become evident as we talk about differences in doctrine and practice in the coming chapters.

5 THE BAPTIST UNDERSTANDING
of the Triune God

Belief in the Trinity is an essential doctrine of Christianity. A correct understanding of the teaching of the triune God is not something that defines a Baptist or a Lutheran. This belief defines a Christian.

Lutherans and Baptists hold the same faith in the triune God. Southern Baptists articulate the Baptist and Christian faith about the Trinity and particularly the second person of the Trinity like this:

Christ is the eternal Son of God. In His incarnation as Jesus Christ he was conceived of the Holy Spirit and born of the virgin Mary. Jesus perfectly revealed and did the will of God, taking upon Himself the demands and necessities of human nature and identifying Himself completely with mankind yet without sin. He honored the divine law by his personal obedience, and in His death on the cross He made provision for the redemption of men from sin. He was raised from the dead with a glorified body and appeared to His disciples as the person who was with them before His crucifixion. He ascended into heaven and is now exalted at the right hand of God where He is the One Mediator, partaking of the nature of God and of man, and in whose Person is effected the reconciliation between God and man. He will return in power and glory to judge the world and to consummate His redemptive mission. He now dwells in all believers as the living and ever present Lord.[55]

Any Lutheran who has confessed the Apostles' Creed or the Nicene Creed recognizes that Baptist belief lines up almost word for word with the ancient creeds of Christendom.

The 1689 Confession of Faith says the same thing in words that echo the Athanasian and Nicene Creeds:

In this divine and infinite Being there are three subsistences, the Father, the Word or Son, and Holy Spirit, of one substance, power, and eternity, each having the whole divine essence, yet the essence undivided: the Father is of none, neither begotten nor proceeding; the Son is eternally begotten of the Father; the Holy Spirit proceeding from the Father and the Son; all infinite, without beginning, therefore but one God, who is not to be divided in nature and being, but distinguished by several peculiar relative properties and personal relations; which doctrine of the Trinity is the foundation of all our communion with God, and comfortable dependence on him.[56]

Lutherans would also agree to the following statement of faith in the Father:

God is the source of all blessings, temporal and spiritual; all that we have and are we owe to Him. Christians have a spiritual debtorship to the whole world, a holy trusteeship in the gospel, and a binding stewardship in their possessions. They are therefore under obligation to serve Him with their time, talents, and material possessions; and should recognize all these as entrusted to them to use for the glory of God and for helping others. According to the Scriptures, Christians should contribute of their means cheerfully, regularly, systematically, proportionately, and liberally for the advancement of the Redeemer's cause on earth.[57]

The same 1689 Confession of Faith quoted above describes the Baptist's understanding of God. Clearly echoing Exodus 34:6,7, the confession describes God as a most pure spirit, invisible, without body, parts, or passions, who only hath immortality, dwelling in the light which no man can approach unto; who is immutable, immense, eternal, incomprehensible, almighty, every way infinite, most holy, most wise, most free, most absolute; working all things according to the counsel of his own immutable and most righteous will for his own glory; most loving, gracious, merciful, long-suffering, abundant in goodness and truth, forgiving iniquity, transgression, and sin; the rewarder of them that diligently seek him, and withal most just and terrible in his judgments, hating all sin, and who will by no means clear the guilty.[58]

6 BAPTIST TEACHING on Conversion

The Bible's word for conversion means to have a change of mind. Picture it as mentally and spiritually turning 180 degrees. We see a soul heading straight toward hell, and something happens to turn that soul around and head it straight toward heaven. The soul has been "converted." A converted person goes from thinking God doesn't matter to thinking God does matter. He matters above everything else! A converted person goes from thinking he owes God nothing to knowing he owes God everything.

Conversion happens when a person comes to realize his sinfulness and how God threatens to punish sinners with an eternity in hell. When that person comes to realize that Jesus has died for the sins of the world, and believes in that forgiveness, the person is converted and made a child of God. The person has gone from darkness to light and from the kingdom of Satan into the kingdom of God.

How is this change worked in us? In this chapter, we want to focus on how the Lutherans' and Baptists' answers to this question differ.

The Lutheran church believes that God gets all the credit for this change of mind and reversal of life's direction. Lutherans believe an unconverted person is in a runaway car, heading for an abyss—no brakes, no steering wheel, no door handles, no chance of getting out. Then God gets into the vehicle with us. He installs brakes and steering and brings the runaway car to a stop, turns it around, and sets it in the right direction—on the road to eternal life with him.

BAPTIST TEACHING ON CONVERSION

Philippians 2:13 says, "It is God who works in you to will and to act according to his good purpose." It is completely an act of God's grace. We don't do anything to get or deserve what God freely gives us. This is what Ephesians chapter 2 says, "It is by grace you have been saved, through faith—and this not from yourselves, it is the gift of God—not by works, so that no one can boast" (verses 8,9). Peter, who surely knew what it was to be helpless in that doomed runaway vehicle, could write to us about our conversion and salvation:

Praise be to the God and Father of our Lord Jesus Christ! In his great mercy he has given us new birth into a living hope through the resurrection of Jesus Christ from the dead, and into an inheritance that can never perish, spoil or fade—kept in heaven for you, who through faith are shielded by God's power until the coming of the salvation that is ready to be revealed in the last time." (1 Peter 1:3-5)

Once a person is a believer and God has worked in him to will and to act according to his good purpose, Lutherans believe that it is possible for that person to participate and cooperate in his life of faith.

Lutheran teaching, nevertheless, emphasizes also the importance and necessity of our cooperation and effort in our sanctification. Unlike Christ's work in justification, the work of the Holy Spirit in sanctification does not substitute for our efforts. It promotes them.[59]

Lutherans don't want to unnecessarily shy away from the word *cooperate*. We do cooperate. We operate alongside the Holy Spirit and serve as those whom the Holy Spirit is empowering. Consider the following Scripture passage: "Do not offer the parts of your body to sin, as instruments of wickedness, but rather offer yourselves to God, as those who have been brought from death to life; and offer the parts of your body to him as instruments of righteousness" (Romans 6:13). In the context of Philippians 2:13 mentioned above, we hear the apostle encourage us to "continue to work out your salvation with fear and trembling" (verse 12). The Holy Spirit is the creator of our faith, but the Holy Spirit does not believe for us. In the same way, God does not do the works of our faith, we do. Yet all the time, he is working in us, "for it is God who works in you to will and to act according to his good purpose" (verse 13).

This understanding helps us recognize the difference between the Lutheran church and the Baptist church with regard to conversion. Lutherans believe that we do not cooperate in our conversion. We are unable to do so. God gets the credit for working conversion—all the credit. Period.

Baptists believe (to a large degree) that we do cooperate in our conversion. God gets most of the credit in conversion, but we get some. We "accept" Christ as our personal Lord and Savior. We invite him into our hearts. We will the change to happen. We ask for it to happen. We declare our intentions.

This reluctance to let God have all the credit characterizes Baptist belief in many respects. According to much Baptist belief, we participate in conversion, doing something for God when we make our choice to accept his invitation. We make the Lord's Supper and Baptism something *we do* for Christ, "an outer manifestation of an inner working" or "an act of obedience." Even prayer is affected. When the marquee says, "Come to our church and get a more successful prayer life," you can see the human element being injected here. If you do it right, you can be successful. The "success" of your prayers depends on you.

This emphasis on helping God and on personal obedience and performance comes from Arminian influences. Professor John Brug makes this point when he says:

> [Jacob Arminius] took issue especially with limited atonement and double predestination. However, when doing this, he fell into the opposite trap of granting to man power to cooperate in his conversion. . . . It is this Wesleyan Arminianism which has characterized much of American Protestantism, especially Methodists and most Baptists.[60]

You can hear this difference between Baptists and Lutherans when you listen to this Baptist statement: "Salvation involves the redemption of the whole man, and is offered freely to all who accept Jesus Christ as Lord and Savior, who by His own blood obtained eternal redemption for the believer."[61] Billy Graham states this belief with reference to the altar call. (Billy Graham is a conservative Southern Baptist clergyman.) He says:

> So faith is not just an emotional reaction, an intellectual realization, or a willful decision; faith is all-inclusive. It involves the intellect, the emotion, and the will. . . .
>
> If you are willing to make this decision and have received Jesus Christ as your own Lord and Savior, then you have become a child of God in whom Jesus Christ dwells.[62]

One of the inconsistencies of the Baptist belief is that it teaches that a person can choose to believe in Jesus, but it believes that once a person is a believer he cannot choose not to believe in Jesus. Actually the ability to choose to believe in Jesus and accept him, which is prevalent in the Baptist church, is at variance with the teaching of irresistible grace and perseverance of the saints. (Recall that Calvin taught that God's grace cannot be resisted, that believers will persevere to the end and do not have the ability to reject Christ.) Billy Graham's call to his hearers to make their decision to accept Jesus Christ as Lord and Savior agrees with Arminian teaching, namely, that we have the power to accept or reject God's grace. The Calvinistic teaching of irresistible grace, coupled with Calvin's teaching of the complete depravity of the human heart, rules out the ability to make a decision to believe, for God will do it all.

The belief of many Baptists that once they are converted and saved they will persevere in faith and salvation is without question the Calvinistic teaching of the perseverance of the saints. Listen to the official statement of the Southern Baptist Convention:

> All true believers endure to the end. Those whom God has accepted in Christ, and sanctified by His Spirit, will

never fall away from the state of grace, but shall persevere to the end. Believers may fall into sin through neglect and temptation, whereby they grieve the Spirit, impair their graces and comforts, bring reproach on the cause of Christ, and temporal judgments on themselves, yet they shall be kept by the power of God through faith unto salvation.[63]

Remember that according to Arminianism, believers have the "freedom to fall eternally." In this case, the official teaching of the Southern Baptist Convention leans toward Calvinism, which teaches that all believers will persevere to the end.

Lutherans believe that it is possible for people to lose their faith. This isn't said to undermine our trust or security, for we know that Jesus has our lives in the palm of his hand and will not allow anyone to snatch us away. Yet the Bible warns us against being complacent in our faith. It warns us against losing faith. In the parable of the sower, Jesus describes one reaction to the gospel like this: "They believe for a while, but in the time of testing they fall away" (Luke 8:13). Hebrews 6:4-6 says:

> It is impossible for those who have once been enlightened, who have tasted the heavenly gift, who have shared in the Holy Spirit, who have tasted the goodness of the word of God and the powers of the coming age, if they fall away, to be brought back to repentance, because to their loss they are crucifying the Son of God all over again and subjecting him to public disgrace.

The apostle Paul speaks about some who lost their faith: "Some have rejected these [truths] and so have shipwrecked their faith. Among them are Hymenaeus and Alexander, whom I have handed over to Satan to be taught not to blaspheme" (1 Timothy 1:19,20). Jesus wrote to the Church in Sardis, "Wake up! Strengthen what remains and is about to die, for I have not found your deeds complete in the sight of my God" (Revelation 3:2). Clearly, Christians can lose their faith and need to watch and pray. At the same time, we can be confident that as members of God's elect, we will never fall away. These two statement are a paradox and cannot stand logically in our minds. But this is what Scripture says. Christians know they need to hear both of these truths.

7
BAPTIST TEACHING on Baptism

Baptists do not refer to Baptism and the Lord's Supper as sacraments, but as Christian *ordinances*. Some Baptists list three ordinances: Baptism, the Lord's Supper, and the washing of feet.

Lutherans speak of the means of grace and list three: Scripture, the Lord's Supper, and Baptism. Through them, God comes to us with his promises and grace. The Lord's Supper and Baptism are identified by Lutherans as sacraments. To qualify as a sacrament according to the Lutheran definition, the practice must (1) use an earthly element, (2) be instituted by God himself, (3) offer the forgiveness of sins.

To Baptists the sacraments are not means of grace in the way Lutherans believe. Baptists are adamant in saying, "Baptism does not save you." Lutherans say, "Yes, it does save you." Twice in 1 Peter 3:20-22 it says just that:

> In it [the ark of Noah] only a few people, eight in all, were saved through water, and this water symbolizes baptism that now saves you also—not the removal of dirt from the body but the pledge of a good conscience toward God. It saves you by the resurrection of Jesus Christ, who has gone into heaven and is at God's right hand—with angels, authorities and powers in submission to him.

And in Titus 3:5-7 God says, "He saved us through the washing of rebirth and renewal by the Holy Spirit, whom he poured out on us generously through Jesus Christ our Savior, so that, having been justified by his grace, we might become heirs having the hope of eternal life." And Jesus told

Nicodemus, "I tell you the truth, no one can enter the kingdom of God unless he is born of water and the Spirit" (John 3:5).

It saddens Lutherans, who value Baptism as such a wonderful act of God, that there even has to be this discussion at all. It is ironic that perhaps the greatest difference between Lutherans and Baptists occurs in the very topic that gives Baptists their name.

The basic difference is, Lutherans believe that in Baptism, God does something wonderful for us. But Baptists believe that in Baptism, we do something wonderful for God. Another way of saying this is that according to Baptist belief, Baptism is part of God's law, but Lutherans say that Baptism works salvation. Baptists label Baptism as "an outer manifestation of an inner working" or "an act of obedience." According to Lutheran belief, Baptism is part of God's gospel, something God does for us.

When Baptists tell people to "accept Christ as personal Lord and Savior" in conversion and then tell people to be baptized and go to the Lord's Supper as acts of obedience, they effectively shift the emphasis from God to man. Calvin denied that the sacraments are means, or instruments, through which God creates and preserves faith. He regarded Baptism and the Lord's Supper merely as outward ceremonies and symbols of what the Holy Spirit does in the heart directly and immediately without means. According to Calvin, Baptism signifies but does not bestow or give new life or forgiveness of sins. In Reformed theology, which is at the root of Baptist teaching, the Lord's Supper is merely a memorial of Christ's death. Lutherans believe the Word, Baptism, and the Lord's Supper are the blessed means of grace![64]

To see the differences between the Lutheran church and the Baptist church in regard to Baptism, we turn to the following statement of belief of the SBC:

> Christian baptism is the immersion of a believer in water in the name of the Father, the Son, and the Holy Spirit. It is *an act of obedience symbolizing* the believer's faith in a

crucified, buried, and risen Savior, the believer's death to sin, the burial of the old life, and the resurrection to walk in newness of life in Christ Jesus. It is a testimony to his faith in the final resurrection of the dead. Being a church ordinance, it is a prerequisite to the privileges of church membership and to the Lord's Supper. [emphasis mine][65]

Regarding the method of administering Baptism, Baptists practice immersion—the complete dunking of a person under water. One of the oldest statements of this belief says:

The way and manner of the dispensing of this Ordinance the Scripture holds out to be dipping or plunging the whole body under water: it being a sign, must answer the thing signified, which are these: First, the washing the whole soul in the blood of Christ; secondly, that interest the Saints have in the death, burial, and resurrection; thirdly, together with a confirmation of our faith, that as certainly as the body is buried under water, and riseth again, so certainly shall the bodies of the Saints be raised by the power of Christ in the day of the resurrection, to reign with Christ. (The word *Baptidzo,* signifying to dip under water, yet so as with convenient garments both upon the administrator and subject, with all modesty.)[66]

Almost all Baptists follow this practice. The American Baptists say:

In light of the fact that the baptism of believers by immersion on their confession of faith in Jesus Christ is a historic and continuing practice among its cooperating churches, the American Baptist Churches in the U.S.A. urges all of its churches to strengthen their witness to this principle in their faith and practice.[67]

Baptists will maintain that there isn't a single instance in Scripture of the Greek word *baptidzo* being used to mean anything other than to immerse. Listen to this statement of the SBC on immersion:

Why Baptists reject sprinkling and pouring for baptism is quite clear. The mode is not New Testament baptism, and lack of it is a perversion of the meaning. But why do Baptists reject the baptism of those who practice immersion for salvation? The same principle applies. Assuming a believer as the subject, New Testament baptism requires both a proper meaning and a proper mode to express that meaning. The meaning is a symbol of Christ's redeeming work for and in the believer. Only immersion expresses that meaning. But even though a group may use the proper mode, if the meaning be sacramental it is still not New Testament baptism. Change the mode and the meaning is lost. Change the meaning and the mode loses its New Testament significance.[68]

Lutherans point out that the Greek word *baptidzo,* according to the dictionary, simply means to apply water in one of four ways: (1) immerse or dunk, (2) sprinkle, (3) wash, (4) pour. Consider the following from a Confessional Lutheran brochure:
The various forms of the word *baptize* occur over one hundred times in the New Testament. The apostle Paul states, "You were washed, you were sanctified, you were justified in the name of the Lord Jesus Christ and by the Spirit of our God" (1 Corinthians 6:11). Notice the picture of washing. It is one of the four basic meanings of the word *baptidzo.* Read carefully, and rejoice. Notice the passive verbs. You were *cleansed.* You were *set apart.* You were *declared innocent before God's throne.* Notice the past tense. It is an accomplished fact. Let skeptics snicker, but no one can change what God has declared."[69]

Lutherans do not say that immersion is wrong. "To immerse is clearly one of the meanings of the Greek word *baptidzo.* But in Mark 7:3,4, the obvious meaning of the word is not to immerse but to apply water in some other way, by pouring or sprinkling:
(The Pharisees and all the Jews do not eat unless they give their hands a ceremonial washing, holding to the tradition

of the elders. When they come from the marketplace they do not eat unless they wash [Greek: *baptidzo*]. And they observe many other traditions, such as the washing [Greek: *baptidzo*] of cups, pitchers and kettles.)

Some texts include "couches." Big kettles and couches could not have routinely and easily been submerged in water. Three thousand people were baptized on Pentecost Day. It stretches the imagination to suppose that there was the ability in the "dry" town of Jerusalem to get three thousand people completely under water in one afternoon.

Regarding infant Baptism, the Baptist catechism deals with the topic like this:

Question 102: Are the infants of professing believers to be baptized?

Answer: The infants of believers are not to be baptized; because there is neither command nor example in the Holy Scriptures, nor implication from them to baptize such.[70]

If, according to Baptist belief, Baptism is "an act of obedience," then it is also possible to understand why Baptists do not baptize infants. According to their belief, infants are not able to make conscious and meaningful decisions that "acts of obedience" demand. Children haven't the verbal ability to declare Jesus Christ as their Lord and Savior, and therefore Baptism would not be something meaningful.

But if, as Lutherans believe, Baptism is God's work and not ours, then it is very easy to understand why infants should be baptized. It is possible to give infants a great gift if God is the giver and they are the recipients. You could give an infant the title to an automobile or establish that infant as the sole heir of a great inheritance. In this case, the goodness and effectiveness of the gift does not depend on the age of the recipient but on the giver.

Lutherans believe Baptism is God's gift to us. He commanded it. He works in it and through it. He puts the power into it. The water is not just simple water but water connected with God's

Word and promise. It is water administered according to the command of the Lord himself. It is done in the name of the Father, Son, and Holy Spirit. After he told the repentant crowd to be baptized for the forgiveness of their sins, Peter told them, "The promise is for you and your children and for all who are far off—for all whom the Lord our God will call" (Acts 2:39). In Acts specific mention is made of the baptism of whole households of people (Cornelius and his family in Acts 10:47,48; Lydia and her household in Acts 16:15; the Philippian jailer and his family in Acts 16:33,34). To be sure, it does not specifically say children were baptized, but it does say "he and his whole family." The burden of proof lies with those who say there weren't children in those households.

Jesus said to his disciples in Matthew 28:19,20, "Therefore go and make disciples of all nations, baptizing them in the name of the Father and of the Son and of the Holy Spirit, and teaching them to obey everything I have commanded you." When he says "all nations," he means just that, everyone in the nation from the youngest to the oldest. The burden of proof again lies with those who say that the normal usage of the word *nation* excludes infants from the command to baptize. There is no arbitrary age at which someone is included in a nation.

When Jesus gave this command to baptize the nations (Matthew 28:19,20), the Jewish culture and religion practiced ritualistic baptism of whole families. Infants and children were commonly brought into Judaism through such baptisms. It was the common practice. It would be unnatural to think that Christ and the apostolic church would have rejected infant Baptism, in common use, without saying a word on the matter. Isn't it much more reasonable to conclude that infant Baptism is not mentioned because it was regarded as a matter of course? When whole families were baptized, everybody understood that the church was simply imitating the practices of the synagogue.[71]

Little children need baptism because they are by nature as sinful as their parents. Lutherans believe that little children are sinful from birth, even from the time of conception. David said in Psalm 51:5, "Surely I was sinful at birth, sinful from the time my mother conceived me."

Listen to Baptist teaching as adopted by the Southern Baptist Convention in 1963:

> Through the temptation of Satan man transgressed the command of God, and fell from his original innocence; whereby his posterity inherit a nature and an environment inclined toward sin, and as soon as they are capable of moral action become transgressors and are under condemnation.[72]

This Baptist statement says that before children are capable of moral action (whenever that might be) they are not sinful.

The senior pastor of one of the fundamentalist churches in the United States, California's Los Gatos Christian Church, reflects Baptist belief in a tract entitled "What About Baptism?"

> The practice of infant christening comes from an old doctrine that babies were guilty of sin inherited from Adam. Therefore, they were christened or *"christianized"* and give a *"christian name."* Now we understand that we become a Christian by receiving Christ as our Savior by faith and then we obey him in immersion or baptism as he commands. *"By grace are ye saved through faith. . . ."* This capacity is beyond the grasp of an infant who is innocent of all sin and needs no christening to make him a Christian.[73]

Consider too what the Free Will Baptists say about this issue:

> We believe that all children dying in infancy, having not actually transgressed against the law of God in their own persons, are only subject to the first death, which was brought on by the fall of the first Adam, and not that any one of them dying in that state shall suffer punishment in hell by the guilt of Adam's sin for of such is the Kingdom of God.[74]

The 1689 Baptist Confession of Faith says this about infants: "Elect infants dying in infancy are regenerated and saved by Christ through the Spirit; who worketh when, and where, and how he pleases; so also are all elect persons, who are incapable of being outwardly called by the ministry of the Word."[75]

These statements of Baptist belief show the conundrum facing people who do not baptize infants. If an infant dies unbaptized, there are only two possibilities. Either the infant died in sin and was lost because he did not yet have faith, or God does something different with the sin of an infant than he does with the sin of an adult. If Baptists are consistent with their own confession, they must believe that the sin of infants necessarily damns them. The 1689 Confession of Faith says this about sin: "There is no sin so small but it deserves damnation."[76]

Lutherans know the wonderful comfort the Bible extends to the parents of children who die in infancy but who were brought to faith through Baptism. Lutheran parents bring their children to the Lord in the same spirit that infants in the Old Testament were brought for circumcision. No little boy ever volunteered for this act or expressed the desire to have it. It was because of his parent's faith that he was there. That had no bearing on whether or not God would work on that child's heart and make him a believing child of Abraham. We bring our children to Baptism knowing that God will work on our children's hearts and bring them to faith.

In Mark chapter 11 Jesus picked up the little children in his arms, put his hands on them, and blessed them. They were blessed by him but not because they had fulfilled this or that law. Their mothers, in faith, brought them to Jesus to have him put his hands on them and bless them. Parents still do that with their little children when they bring them to be baptized. Lutherans believe that if Jesus could bless infants in his day, he can still bless little children through his gift of Baptism.

The August 2001 issue of *The Berean Call* contains the following warning from a reader of that publication. The man who speaks had once been a Lutheran but has become a Baptist. This warning states the difference between Baptists and Lutherans in a very pointed way:

> You must know that Luther's Catechism, used by every Lutheran Synod, declares concerning the "Sacrament of Baptism," that "it works forgiveness of sins, delivers from death and the devil, and gives eternal salvation to all who believe this, as the words and promises of God declare." It also states regarding the "Sacrament of the Altar," that "in the Sacrament forgiveness of sins, life, and salvation are given us through these words."
>
> This false sacramental gospel kept my parents from ever telling me that I was a sinner and needed a Savior. They thought that I had received eternal life in baptism. I am positive that there are millions of Lutherans believing the same thing my parents did and which I was taught and believed for many years.
>
> I was saved at age 45 when I finally heard the true gospel and believed it. Martin Luther protested some of the obvious errors and corruption in the Catholic Church, but kept the sacraments as the means of grace by which a person must be saved. This is taught from his Catechism in every Lutheran Church today.
>
> Furthermore, like the Roman Catholics, both Luther and Calvin and their followers at that time persecuted our true spiritual forefathers, the Anabaptists, who refused to submit to baby baptism or to acknowledge the physical presence of Christ in the bread and wine at the Lord's Table.[77]

It seems that this man's parents misused God's gift of Baptism by not pointing out the daily blessing of Baptism. Members of God's family daily drown the old sinful nature through contrition and repentance. This misuse led the man to accept the Baptist teaching of believer's baptism. This serves as a warning for Lutheran parents not to forget what Baptism has done for their children and to remind them of it often.

8 BAPTIST TEACHING on the Lord's Supper

The difference between Lutherans and Baptists on the Lord's Supper boils down to one thing: what does the word *is* mean? Jesus didn't say the bread represented his body. He said the bread *is* his body. Jesus didn't say the cup of wine represented his blood. He said the cup *is* blood. Lutherans believe that in the Lord's Supper, Jesus' true body and blood are really present with the bread and the wine. This teaching regarding the Lord's Supper is called the Real Presence.[78] It takes the words of Jesus literally when he said, "This is my body, which is for you. . . . This cup is the new covenant in my blood" (1 Corinthians 11:24,25). In this reference Scripture clearly says that he took the bread and then he took the cup. With bread in his hand he said, "This is my body." With the wine in his hand he said, "This cup is the new covenant in my blood."

Luther wrote:

Let a hundred thousand devils, with all the fanatics, rush forward and say, "How can bread and wine be Christ's body and blood?" Still I know that all the spirits and scholars put together have less wisdom than the divine Majesty has in his little finger. Here we have Christ's word, "Take, eat; this is my body." "Drink of it, all of you, this is the new covenant in my blood," etc. Here we shall take our stand and see who dares to instruct Christ and alter what he has spoken.[79]

Calvin and his allies (including many Baptists) understood Christ's words in an entirely different manner. They declare:

We repudiate as preposterous interpreters, those who in the solemn words of the Supper, "This is My body, this is My blood," urge a precisely literal sense, as they say. For we hold it to be indisputable that these words are to be accepted figuratively, so that bread and wine are called that which they signify.[80]

Calvin on the basis of his rationalistic principles, thought that Luther was "preposterous" because he accepted Christ's sacred words at face value. Because Calvin could not comprehend how bread and wine could be the true body and blood of Jesus Christ, he simply would not believe it.[81]

The Southern Baptist Convention says this about the Lord's Supper:

[It] is a symbolic act of obedience whereby members of the church, through partaking of the bread and the fruit of the vine, memorialize the death of the Redeemer and anticipate His second coming.[82]

"Baptists believe that the elements merely symbolize the body and blood of Jesus, with no saving effect in partaking of them." So says Herschel Hobbs in his description of the teaching of the SBC.[83] Hobbs goes on to elaborate on Baptist belief:

When Jesus said, "This is my body" and "this is my blood" (Matthew 26:26,28) he no more meant that they actually became such than by saying, "I am the door" (John 10:9), he meant that he was a hole in a wall or a piece of wood. In all cases he spoke symbolically. So the elements are merely symbols of his body and blood. Like the meaning in baptism, the elements portray that which Jesus did for man's salvation. Both are visual aids whereby the believer portrays the basis and experience of his saving relationship with Jesus Christ. . . . Both ordinances are sermons in symbol of Jesus' redeeming work and promised return.[84]

Note that in Hobbs' thinking, the Lord's Supper is entirely something the believer does for God rather than a sacrament through which God does something for us—namely, giving us the forgiveness of sins.

When Jesus calls himself a door, it is clear that he is using a figure of speech. Jesus is indeed a door. The dictionary says that a door is "any way to go in or out." Jesus said, "No one comes to the Father except through me" (John 14:6). Jesus did not say that he is symbolized by a door. He said that he is a door. Jesus is not a symbol of something that gets us into heaven. He is that way into heaven. He is that door.

Traditionally Lutherans have practiced close(d) Communion. In the Lord's Supper, the communicant enjoys fellowship with God. Communicants, however, also practice fellowship with one another. It has always been Lutheran belief that for this communion to be a real sharing (which is what the word *communion* means), the people who share in the Lord's Supper must also share a common faith.

Jesus instituted his Lord's Supper in the close company of his disciples in the upper room in Jerusalem on the night he was betrayed. Those in attendance had been with him in fellowship and teaching for three years. It was in this intimate setting that the Lord gave his command, "This cup is the new covenant in my blood; do this, whenever you drink it, in remembrance of me" (1 Corinthians 11:25). In 1 Corinthians chapter 11, the Lord's Supper is discussed and explained in the context of the congregational life at Corinth. Paul says that each communicant should examine himself before he comes to the Lord's Supper. This implies an understanding of the Christian faith—of Jesus' sacrifice for us and of what is present in the Lord's Supper. Paul also told the Corinthians to come to the Lord Supper with the realization that the people next to them shared in the same faith.

Insofar as the Baptist churches today follow the 1689 Confession of Faith, they agree with the practice of close(d) Communion. In chapter 30, "Of the Lord's Supper," paragraph 1, we read that the Lord's Supper is to be a bond and pledge of their communion with him, and with each other. . . . All ignorant and ungodly persons, as they are unfit to enjoy communion with Christ, so are they unworthy of the Lord's table, and cannot, without great sin against him, while they remain such, partake of these holy mysteries, or be admitted thereunto; yea, whosoever shall receive unworthily, are guilty of the body and blood of the Lord, eating and drinking judgment to themselves.

The Lutheran practice of close(d) Communion is not an attempt to be unfriendly or exclusive. It gives the visitor to the congregation the chance to determine whether he or she really is of one mind and heart with those who are celebrating the Lord's Supper in that particular place. It also gives the pastor the ability to examine the communicants to ascertain whether those receiving the Lord's Supper are able to receive the Lord's blessing of salvation there and not be harmed spiritually or come under God's judgment (see 1 Corinthians 11:27-30).

Hershel Hobbs represents Baptist belief about the concept of close(d) Communion by saying:

A brief word should be said about the charge that Baptists are "closed communionists." To begin with, the Lord's Supper is not communion between men but between the believer and the Lord. . . . New Testament baptized believers are eligible to take the Lord's Supper. Some Baptist churches hold that one should be a member of the church in which he partakes of it, holding that he should be in the fellowship and under the discipline of the church which administers it. Most Baptist churches hold that any member of any Baptist church is eligible.[85]

The difference in practice between Baptists and Lutherans is clear.

9 BAPTISTS ON MARRIAGE *and family*

Today the traditional family and the institution of marriage have been assaulted as never before. The issues discussed are ones that would have been unthinkable to Lutheran and Baptist believers of the past. The very definition of marriage and family is being tampered with. Churches are debating same-sex marriage. Then there is the homosexual question, with some so-called Christian churches having practicing homosexuals among their clergy. Homosexual couples are raising children and calling themselves a family.

The 2000 "Baptist Faith and Message" of the SBC sums up the basic belief of Baptists (which Lutherans hold too) regarding marriage and children when it says:

Marriage is the uniting of one man and one woman in covenant commitment for a lifetime. It is God's unique gift to reveal the union between Christ and His church and to provide for the man and the woman in marriage the framework for intimate companionship, the channel of sexual expression according to biblical standards, and the means for procreation of the human race.

The husband and wife are of equal worth before God, since both are created in God's image. The marriage relationship models the way God relates to His people. A husband is to love his wife as Christ loved the church. He has the God-given responsibility to provide for, to protect, and to lead his family. A wife is to submit herself graciously to the servant leadership of her husband even as the church willingly submits to the headship of Christ.

She, being in the image of God as is her husband and thus equal to him, has the God-given responsibility to respect her husband and to serve as his helper in managing the household and nurturing the next generation.

Children, from the moment of conception, are a blessing and heritage from the Lord. Parents are to demonstrate to their children God's pattern for marriage. Parents are to teach their children spiritual and moral values and to lead them, through consistent lifestyle example and loving discipline, to make choices based on biblical truth. Children are to honor and obey their parents.[86]

In 1689 the Baptist believers said this about marriage:
It is lawful for all sorts of people to marry, who are able with judgment to give their consent; yet it is the duty of Christians to marry in the Lord; and therefore such as profess the true religion, should not marry with infidels, or idolaters; neither should such as are godly, be unequally yoked, by marrying with such as are wicked in their life, or maintain damnable heresy.[87]

To what degree that statement was enforced back when the confession was written, we don't know. Neither the Baptist church (nor the Lutheran church) today has "laws" against religious intermarriage. Both churches would certainly agree, however, with the wisdom of the 1689 statement.

The SBC's position on sexuality says:
We affirm God's plan for marriage and sexual intimacy— one man, and one woman, for life. Homosexuality is not a "valid alternative lifestyle." The Bible condemns it as sin. It is not, however, unforgivable sin. The same redemption available to all sinners is available to homosexuals. They, too, may become new creations in Christ.[88]

The Baptist and Lutheran churches agree with the epistle to the Romans in its condemnation of the perversion of practicing homosexuals:

Even their women exchanged natural relations for unnatural ones. In the same way the men also abandoned natural relations with women and were inflamed with lust for one another. Men committed indecent acts with other men, and received in themselves the due penalty for their perversion. (Romans 1:26,27)

Certainly both churches understand that repentant homosexuals are welcome and are to be invited into the Lord's fellowship of the sinners and saints. It must be said that within the Baptist and Lutheran churches (although not in conservative Lutheran churches) there are those who follow the god of this age and seek to find ways of justifying homosexuality and even celebrating it. Yet this is still the exception to the rule.

The Baptist Statement of Belief quoted above says this about life: "Children, from the moment of conception, are a blessing and heritage from the Lord." The phrase "from the moment of conception" defines both Baptist and Lutheran belief regarding unborn babies and abortion. This belief leads to the following statement: "In the spirit of Christ, Christians should . . . speak on behalf of the unborn and contend for the sanctity of all human life from conception to natural death."[89]

When King David, the slayer of Goliath and the champion also of babies, spoke in Psalm 139, he spoke for us all:

I praise you because I am fearfully and wonderfully made; your works are wonderful, I know that full well. My frame was not hidden from you when I was made in the secret place. When I was woven together in the depths of the earth, your eyes saw my unformed body. All the days ordained for me were written in your book before one of them came to be. (verses 14-16)

When those who believe in the infallible and inspired Word of God hear those verses, they join Lutherans and Baptists in condemning abortion, which stops a beating heart and cuts short the days that God ordained for that child.

In 1904, a simpler and more straightforward time, Baptists said this about divorce:

WHEREAS, The facility with which divorces are at present obtained in our courts is an incentive to exaggerate the minor difficulties of married life, and an encouragement to dissolve the union that otherwise would continue with difficulties removed; and

WHEREAS, The laws of our States, with a few exceptions, permit divorces for many and often trivial cases; therefore

RESOLVED, That it is the sense of this body that the Legislatures of the States represented in this Convention be requested to discourage this great and growing evil by more stringent laws regulating the same

RESOLVED, That it is the sense of this body that Baptist ministers should refuse to solemnize the rites of matrimony in cases where one or both parties concerned have been divorced on other than Scriptural grounds, as laid down in Matthew 19:9.[90]

A summary of Lutheran belief on marriage and divorce says this:

God joins the husband and wife together in marriage; God dissolves such a union through death. Whenever man puts asunder what God has joined together, sin is involved. Through fornication and malicious desertion the marriage bond is broken. A divorce by the court may be secured to establish this legally. Under any other circumstances, the divorce itself breaks the marriage and is contrary to Scripture.[91]

Both Baptists and Lutherans believe that Malachi 2:16 still stands: "'I hate divorce,' says the LORD God of Israel, 'and I hate a man's covering himself with violence as well as with his garment,' says the LORD Almighty." In this same chapter and context, God says this about marriage and divorce: "Has not the LORD made them [the married couple] one? . . . And why one? Because he was seeking godly offspring. So guard yourself in your spirit, and do not break faith with the wife of your youth" (verse 15).

And of course Jesus' words still stand, which say, "I tell you that anyone who divorces his wife, except for marital unfaithfulness, and marries another woman commits adultery" (Matthew 19:9).

10
THE BAPTISTS' LIFE OF FAITH
and Good Works

Both Lutheran and Baptist churches teach that believers in Jesus are saved by grace, through faith, without any deeds of righteousness on our part contributing to our salvation. The Bible is surely clear on that. "It is by grace you have been saved, through faith—and this not from yourselves, it is the gift of God—not by works, so that no one can boast" (Ephesians 2:8,9). The Bible speaks about our natural selves as being "dead in . . . transgressions and sins" (Ephesians 2:1). We cannot contribute to our rebirth or to our final salvation.

The Baptist 1689 Statement of Belief says:

Man, by his fall into a state of sin, hath wholly lost all ability of will to any spiritual good accompanying salvation; so as a natural man, being altogether averse from that good, and dead in sin, is not able by his own strength to convert himself, or to prepare himself thereunto.[92]

Calvin believed this. So did Martin Luther. This effectively points out the error of the Arminian segment of the Baptist church, which teaches that all people have within themselves the ability to decide for or against God's offer of salvation.

But, like Calvin, the Calvinistic segment of the Baptist church quickly goes on to teach double predestination, that is, that God predestined some to eternal life and some to eternal death.

Lutherans can agree with the following words:

Those whom God hath predestinated unto life, he is pleased in his appointed, and accepted time, effectually to call, by his Word and Spirit, out of that state of sin and death in which they are by nature, to grace and salvation by Jesus Christ; enlightening their minds spiritually and savingly to understand the things of God; taking away their heart of stone, and giving unto them a heart of flesh; renewing their wills, and by his almighty power determining them to that which is good, and effectually drawing them to Jesus Christ; yet so as they come most freely, being made willing by his grace.[93]

Lutherans cannot, however, agree with a double predestination in which the will of God expressed above in regard to the elect is not his will regarding all people. That God does not predestine some to be damned is clear from such passages as 1 Timothy 2:3,4: "This is good, and pleases God our Savior, who wants all men to be saved and to come to a knowledge of the truth." Another passage that clearly speaks against double predestination is 2 Corinthians 5:19, "God was reconciling the world to himself in Christ, not counting men's sins against them. And he has committed to us the message of reconciliation." God's message of grace is intended for all people.

Good works, however, do follow when a person is converted. Listen to the following Baptist confession regarding the good works that must follow a Christian's conversion:

Good works are only such as God hath commanded in his Holy Word, and not such as without the warrant thereof are devised by men out of blind zeal, or upon any pretence of good intentions. These good works, done in obedience to God's commandments, are the fruits and evidences of a true and lively faith; and by them believers manifest their thankfulness, strengthen their assurance, edify their brethren, adorn the profession of the gospel, stop the mouths of the adversaries, and glorify God, whose workmanship they are, created in Christ Jesus thereunto, that having their fruit unto holiness they may have the end eternal life. Their ability to do good works is not at all of themselves, but wholly from the Spirit of Christ; and that they may be enabled thereunto, besides the graces they have already received, there is necessary an actual influence of the same Holy Spirit, to work in them to will and to do of his good pleasure; yet they are not hereupon to grow negligent, as if they were not bound to perform any duty, unless upon a special motion of the Spirit, but they ought to be diligent in stirring up the grace of God that is in them.[94]

Lutherans would say "Amen!" to that. Good works are necessary to salvation only as evidence that faith is present. James says, "Faith by itself, if it is not accompanied by action, is dead" (2:17). James goes on to say about Abraham and his faith, "You see that his faith and his actions were working together, and his faith was made complete by what he did" (2:22).

Christians live a godly life. They must. God is at work in them "to will and to act according to his good purpose" (Philippians 2:13). The works God would have us do were ordained before the world began (Ephesians 2:8-10). Lutherans want to stress salvation by grace alone without the deeds of the law, and rightfully so. But the life of a Christian and the stress the New Testament epistles place on living the life of faith must not allow Christians to downplay in any way the active and evident Christian life of faith.

We can certainly agree with these words of a Baptist pastor: Reformed Baptist churches are distinguished by the conviction that salvation radically alters the life of the convert. It is tragic that such a thing needs to be mentioned. We live in the day of decisionism. The idea is that you pray a certain formula prayer and that you are therefore declared to be saved. It matters not whether you break with sin or pursue holiness (Hebrews 12:14). You can live like hell and go to heaven! What a bargain! Many popular Bible teachers declare this as the great defense of the grace of God. . . . The Jesus we proclaim is a great Savior. He does not leave His people in their lifeless condition. We proclaim the Jesus who came to save his people FROM their sins (Matthew 1:21). We proclaim the biblical truth that if anyone is in Christ he is a new creature (2 Corinthians 5:17). We proclaim the Jesus who came to make a people zealous for good works (Titus 2:14).[95]

A faithful and fervent life of worship is one of the fruits of a Christian's life. The book of Hebrews commands, "Let us not give up meeting together, as some are in the habit of doing, but let us encourage one another—and all the more as you see the Day approaching" (10:25). Martin Luther said in his catechism with regard to the Third Commandment, "We should fear and love God that we do not despise preaching and his Word, but regard it as holy and gladly hear and learn it."[96]

Baptist Pastor Savistio agrees, perhaps at the risk of becoming a bit legalistic, though:

There ought not to be a great disparity between Sunday morning and evening and mid week. The same membership is expected to be at all the services of the church. It is impossible to share in the life of the church in the manner which God intended and to willingly absent yourself from its public gatherings. We recognize that few churches would make such a demand, but biblical churchmanship presupposes such a commitment to God, your pastors, and your brothers and sisters.[97]

A resolution of the Southern Baptist Convention expresses their ideas about the Sabbath—the Lord's Day:

WHEREAS, The Creation account recorded in Genesis 2:1-13 states that God completed His work of Creation in six days and rested on the seventh day; and

WHEREAS, The Fourth Commandment [the Third Commandment by Lutheran reckoning] recognizes the importance of keeping one day holy; and

WHEREAS, Jesus by example and teaching kept one day for worship; and

WHEREAS, Since much of the moral breakdown in our society has come since keeping the Lord's Day holy has been largely disregarded.

Therefore, Be it RESOLVED, That this 135th session of the Southern Baptist Convention affirms the biblical teaching concerning the Lord's Day as a matter of faith and practice; and

Be it further RESOLVED, That we urge Southern Baptist churches to teach the importance of the proper use of the Lord's Day to strengthen families and give proper recognition to God as Creator; and

Be it finally RESOLVED, That Southern Baptists express concern over the continuing secularization of the Lord's Day.[98]

We too must fight the secularization of Sunday. These days it is hard to ignore the many activities that communities and schools schedule on Sunday in direct competition with Sunday worship services. It used to be in Baptist strongholds like Texas that Sundays were considered by secular school authorities as "sacred." (Wednesday evenings were too.) No more. Now soccer tournaments and school band contests are scheduled on Sundays with impunity. In the workplace too, weekends are seen as good times to schedule mandatory seminars and workshops.

Without emphasizing Sunday as the particular day on which one must worship, Lutherans remember what Luther did say in regard to the Third Commandment. He said people who regularly miss church because of other scheduled activities are in strong danger of despising preaching and the Word. Lutherans sometimes schedule worship services on Thursday or Saturday evenings to make it possible for busy people (and maybe distracted people) to attend worship regularly.

We should, however, point out the difference between Baptists and Lutherans with regard to prayer. The Lutheran belief about prayer is stated well by Professor John Brug of Wisconsin Lutheran Seminary. He says:

> We do not confuse prayer with the means of grace as many other Protestants do. Because prayer is our act toward God, we cannot place it on the same level as the means of grace, which are God's gracious speaking to us. Nevertheless, we can and should pray for strength and guidance in sanctification, both for ourselves and for others.[99]

The New Testament tells believers to pray without ceasing. The disciples came to Jesus and asked to be taught how to pray. Christians pray the Lord's Prayer regularly. Martin Luther gave Lutherans his "Morning Prayer" and "Evening Prayer." The epistle of James tells us that we don't have, because we haven't prayed (4:2). James points to Elijah and says, "Elijah was a man just like us. He prayed earnestly that it would not rain, and it did not rain on the land for three and a half years. Again he prayed, and the heavens gave rain, and the earth produced its crops" (5:17,18). And of course, the greatest example of one who prayed is our Lord himself, who went by himself to lonely places to be with his Father in prayer. It was the last thing he did before he died. His words from the cross were essentially prayers to his heavenly Father, just as we hope that our last words will be prayers to our heavenly Father.

Lutherans do value and treasure prayer. But Lutherans do not believe that prayer is a means of grace. Lutherans believe that prayer is a fruit of faith. When we ask the Lord to give us his Holy Spirit, to create faith in a person's heart or to sustain and strengthen our faith, the Lord answers those prayers through the means of grace. But prayer itself is not one of the means through which God gives us his Holy Spirit.

Baptists, however, make prayer a way faith is created and nurtured. They give prayer a power that goes beyond its already great power to ask God for his blessings. The

Calvinists paved the way for this thinking about prayer when they said in the Westminster Confession (XIV, 1):

> The grace of faith, whereby the elect are enabled to believe to the saving of their souls, is the work of the Spirit of Christ in their hearts, and is ordinarily wrought by the ministry of the Word, by which also, and by the administration of the Sacraments *and prayer,* it is increased and strengthened [italics added].[100]

Note that the sacraments and prayer are put on the same level, both serving to increase and strengthen faith.

Billy Graham represents Baptist belief about prayer when he teaches the "sinner's prayer" in his book *How to Be Born Again*. Billy Graham leads people who are not yet believers to pray:

> O God, I acknowledge that I have sinned against You. I am sorry for my sins. I am willing to turn from my sins. I openly receive and acknowledge Jesus Christ as my Savior. I confess Him as Lord. From this moment on I want to live for Him and serve Him. In Jesus' name. Amen.[101]

Graham goes on to say, "If you are willing to make this decision and have received Jesus Christ as your Lord and Savior, then you have become a child of God in whom Jesus Christ dwells." Prayer thus becomes the means by which and through which Christ becomes the seeker's Savior.

11

BAPTIST CHURCH *Organization*

Both Baptists and Lutherans used to be puzzled when they said the Apostles' Creed and heard the words "the holy catholic Church." Not many Lutheran churches use that version of the Apostles' Creed anymore. Today we say "the holy Christian Church." The word *catholic,* as it was used there, means the universal church of believers in Jesus Christ.

Baptists define the church this way:

The catholic or universal church, which (with respect to the internal work of the Spirit and truth of grace) may be called invisible, consists of the whole number of the elect, that have been, are, or shall be gathered into one, under Christ, the head thereof; and is the spouse, the body, the fullness of him that filleth all in all.[102]

Lutherans similarly say, "[The Holy Spirit] calls, gathers, enlightens, and sanctifies the whole Christian church on earth, and keeps it with Jesus Christ in the one true faith."[103] This is the invisible church, the church that only the Holy Spirit knows.

So Baptists and Lutherans agree on what is meant by the universal church of Christ. Yet, as we have seen in chapter 3, there is a difference in emphasis between Baptists and Lutherans regarding the creeds and the external organization in physical, visible churches. Lutherans value a synodical organization more than Baptists do because they look to their synod to take action against churches that depart from Lutheran teaching. Baptists, however, value creeds less than Lutherans, and they see their denomination taking less of a role in doctrinal issues.

However, when Baptist congregations cross whatever doctrinal or church practice line their denomination chooses to establish, they often operate much the same as Lutherans. Their attitude is summed up in a statement from the official Web page of the Southern Baptist Convention:

> We affirm the autonomy of the local church. Each church is free to determine its own membership and to set its own course under the headship of Jesus. It may enter into alliance with other churches as it chooses, so long as those other churches are willing. The same is true for other Baptist bodies—local associations; state conventions; national conventions. They, too, may determine their membership and set their own course. If, in its autonomy, a Baptist body expels a church from its fellowship, it does not negate that church's autonomy. The church is perfectly free to go on with its business—but not as a member of that larger Baptist body.[104]

Herschel Hobbs points out another area where Baptists and Lutherans share common ground: "An adequate system of Christian schools is necessary to a complete spiritual program for Christ's people."[105] Lutherans have from the beginning valued Christian education. In the yearly annuals of Lutheran churches, the list of active teachers rivals in number the list of active pastors, which is hardly true of most other denominations.

It may be that the emerging preschool phenomenon in both Baptist and Lutheran churches to minister to working mothers and single parents will spark a resurgence of interest and importance congregations place on Christian education. Let's hope that this will be the case. "Train a child in the way he should go, and when he is old he will not turn from it" (Proverbs 22:6) is still the biblical word on Christian education.

Women pastors and preachers is a question guaranteed to stir up controversy and conversation among Baptists and Lutherans alike. It can also generally be said about both church bodies that those who are more liberal in theology have women pastors and preachers and those who are conservative do not. Among Lutherans, for instance, the Evangelical Lutheran Church in America (ELCA) boldly admits on its official Web page that on a continuum of all churches in the United States from the very conservative to the very liberal, the ELCA is on the most liberal end. On this same Web page appear various ELCA women pastors with bios attached. The more conservative of the Lutheran churches (The Lutheran Church—Missouri Synod, the Wisconsin Evangelical Lutheran Synod, the Evangelical Lutheran Synod) are very clear in stating their belief that Scripture clearly limits the pastoral and preaching ministry to men.

The following is representative of conservative Lutheran churches on the question of women in the public and pastoral ministry:

> The Lord teaches us through His Word that women are not given the responsibility of serving the church as pastors. . . . God has given His church many gifts. Among them is the gift of the office of the public, pastoral ministry. We receive what God gives, in the way He has given it, and in the form He has given it. . . . The church which wishes to remain faithful to the Word of God cannot permit the ordination of women to the pastoral office.[106]

The conservative Baptists have the same stance. The Reformed Baptists say:

> Reformed Baptists are distinguished by a conviction regarding male leadership in the church. Our age has witnessed the feminization of Christianity. God created two sexes in creation and gave to each different corresponding roles. While the sexes are equal in Creation, the Fall, and in Redemption God has nonetheless sovereignly ordained that leadership in the home, the state, and the church is to be male. It is our experience that those whose minds have been unduly influenced by this generation find our worship, leadership, and family

structure to be jarring. When the Bible speaks of husbands and fathers leading the home (see Eph. 5,6, and Col. 3) it is not culturally conditioned. When the Bible speaks of men leading in prayer, teaching, preaching, and serving as elders and deacons we must bow with submissive and dutiful hearts. Culture must not carry the day in the church of Jesus Christ![107]

The Southern Baptists say, "While both men and women are gifted for service in the church, the office of pastor is limited to men as qualified by Scripture."[108] This is official doctrine. You can hear some softening of this, however, when you read the following from a recent Southern Baptist publication regarding this issue:

> For all the articles regarding women pastors published by both secular and religious publications in the weeks preceding the annual convention, the only mention of such was Rogers' reference to the subject in citing the revised statement: "The convention has spoken clearly its conviction that while both men and women are gifted and called for ministry, the office of pastor is limited to men as qualified by Scripture."
>
> Questions regarding women pastors arose in a news conference immediately following the vote on the statement. There, Rogers was quick to note a preliminary study done by Midwestern Baptist Theological Seminary in Kansas City, Mo., which shows that only one-tenth of 1 percent of Southern Baptist churches have women as pastors (or a total of 35 or less churches among the overall 40,000-plus SBC churches). Rogers said that in no way does the document, particularly the section on the pastorate, dictate who a Southern Baptist church may hire as pastor.[109]

An example of the "one-tenth of 1 percent of Southern Baptist churches" that do have a woman as pastor was discussed in chapter 3. Even though Southern Baptists as a group hold to the principal of male leadership in the church, they do allow women into the pulpits of Southern Baptist churches. They are training them for this.

Chuck Kelley, committee member and president of New Orleans Baptist Theological Seminary, added that more women are now being trained for ministry in Southern Baptist seminaries than at any other time in the SBC's history.[110]

The more liberal American Baptists almost champion the issue of women suffrage in the churches:

Another arena of our growing inclusiveness is illustrated by the history of women within our denomination: a record of service and an account of struggle to gain the right of full participation. The Woman's Home Mission Society and the Woman's Foreign Mission Society were founded to sponsor single women on the mission field and to meet the specific needs of women and children. When the woman's mission societies merged with their counterparts (the American Baptist Home Mission Society and the American Baptist Foreign Mission Society) in 1955, women's struggles for opportunities for leadership and service intensified. Efforts to include women in every facet of denominational life and leadership have spawned a host of resolutions, commissions, task forces and studies to address the need for the full partnership of women.[111]

CONCLUSION AND APPLICATIONS

This book began with the goal of giving a fair representation of both Baptist and Lutheran beliefs. This has been a difficult task, considering the variety of Baptist beliefs among the churches who call themselves Baptist. There are only generalities and general statements of confession and belief.

In a number of instances Baptists and Lutherans can rejoice because they believe the same things. And what they agree on are important teachings of Scripture. The verbal inspiration of Scripture, salvation by grace, the importance of living the Christian faith and life are some examples. But there are times when Lutherans cannot rejoice, times when differences cause grief. There is no way to be happy when a Christian looks at the Bible and comes away with a wrong interpretation and conclusion.

Baptists and Lutherans have a different spirit. This difference was noted by Martin Luther when in Marburg, Germany, in 1529, he met with Uhlrich Zwingli (who shared many beliefs with John Calvin and with the later Baptists). Martin Luther came away from the colloquy saying that they *"haben einen anderen Geist"* ("have a different spirit").

If you examine all the differences in Lutheran and Baptist teaching, most of them rest on several basic things. Baptist church bodies, with their various mixtures of Calvinism and Arminianism, stress man's involvement—in Baptism, the Lord's Supper, conversion, and prayer. Lutherans say that the emphasis in all these elements of our faith must remain with God and what he does for us. There was also a great difference between Calvin and Luther on the proper interpretation of

Scripture. The Calvinists leaned toward the idea that Scripture spoke metaphorically, rationally, and figuratively. They did not want Scripture to say anything irrational. Lutherans said that Scripture interprets Scripture and that the exact and literal interpretation should be followed wherever and whenever possible, even when this goes against human reason. From these two main differences come all the others.

Lutherans do not do their Baptist friends a service by agreeing to disagree. The differences are real, and they are very important. The differences can alter, weaken, and even destroy faith. Lutherans want to continue to study Scripture and base their faith on Scripture alone.

A Practical Approach to a Baptist Friend

The purpose of this book is not just to give us an intellectual understanding of Baptists. The purpose of the book is to give us knowledge that we can apply in helping and counseling Baptist friends and neighbors. We Lutherans want to be able to help them understand Scripture correctly and to have the purest belief and trust in what Jesus has done for them.

Imagine the following scenario: You have spoken with your neighbor a number of times over your backyard fence. You wave at him when he pulls into his driveway. He greets you when he goes out to check his mailbox. So you have this casual acquaintance. One day you decide to take the plunge, and you say, "You know, I was wondering what church you go to. I'm a Lutheran and I love Jesus and I was wondering if you are a Christian too." Something like that. Your neighbor might say, "Sure, I'm a Christian. I'm a Baptist."

Over time you become closer friends with your Baptist neighbor. He trusts you enough to share with you his worries and concerns. Maybe he loses his job. Maybe his wife is diagnosed with cancer. Maybe his children are in trouble. Something is happening to shake him in his faith. You want to help your neighbor as Jonathan helped David in the Old Testament. Jonathan "helped [David] find strength in God"

(1 Samuel 23:16). You want to help your neighbor find strength in the Lord. Real friends do that.

If you understand some things about the Baptist religious experience, you can help your neighbor. Hopefully, you have learned some of these things by reading this book. The information you have gleaned will put you in good stead as you speak about your faith to your friend. We want to be good witnesses to God's truth and to speak this truth in love to everyone who will listen to us.

You wonder what's going on in your neighbor's mind? How does this person see things spiritually? What is his strength? What is his weakness? What is he feeling . . . and why? You know you must find out about your friend.

It could very well be that before you ask your Baptist neighbor about his faith and where he goes to church, he has already asked you about yours. This might be more the rule than the exception. Lutherans aren't known for being particularly good at evangelism and talking quickly to others about their Savior and their faith in him. This is a generalization of course. But your Baptist neighbor may not be so shy about talking about his faith.

Baptists often have the courage to approach you on the street and ask you if you have received Jesus into your own life as your personal Savior. That isn't an easy thing to do. As a matter of fact, it is hard. Maybe the first thing we should realize about talking to Baptists is that your Baptist neighbor may not be reluctant to talk about his faith in Jesus and his church's beliefs.

There is a second thing you might notice. Your Baptist neighbor may have a Bible that's well worn. As you start to talk about your beliefs, he may say, "Wait just a second. Let me go get my Bible." When he comes out of the house with his Bible in hand, take a close look at it. You can tell a great deal about a person by looking at his Bible. Someone once said, "If you see someone whose Bible is coming apart, you can be pretty sure his life isn't." Many Baptists love their Bibles and use them

CONCLUSION AND APPLICATIONS

a lot. They wear them out. They love to study their Bibles. They mark them up. They know where proof passages are. (This sometimes makes it kind of intimidating to talk to them.) They come from churches in which the "sermon" is often really a Bible study. The preacher steps before them and goes through a section of Scripture verse by verse.

When the Bible of the person we are talking to is worn, it is an encouraging thing. In fact, before you talk to a person about the Bible, you should find out if he accepts the Bible as the inspired Word of God. Has this person done what we Lutherans say, "Read, mark, learn, and inwardly digest" the Bible?

If you have this assurance, you can proceed meaningfully with your discussion. If this is not so—if the person doesn't believe that the Bible is inspired by God and true—then it becomes difficult to go further. It may become hard to counsel or advise your neighbor. At that point you would have to explain the basics, and ask the Lord to give you an opening to talk about your sin and the grace God has given you in Christ.

In general, though, you will find yourself in agreement with your Baptist neighbor that the Bible is verbally inspired. Your neighbor might not interpret the words on the Bible page as you do—as you have learned, Baptists misapply many Scripture verses—but you can rejoice that you have this common starting point in all your discussions.

On the same note, make sure your Baptist friend knows that you believe that Scripture is inspired. Many Baptists classify all Lutherans as liberal (which, of course, many in the ELCA are). Assure them that you believe the Bible is inspired and inerrant, as they do.

As you discuss the Bible, you will want to keep reminding your neighbor as you go along, "What do these words say? What is the simplest, easiest, and most obvious way to understand these words? Let's let God be God and listen carefully to what he says."

Don't be surprised if somewhere along the line your Baptist neighbor asks you when you became a Christian. If you came to faith later in life, most likely you will be able to give him a general answer. Most likely, you came to faith when you were baptized. Your neighbor will not be satisfied with that answer. He may respond, "No, I mean when did you really come to know Jesus?"

If you ask your Baptist neighbor the same question, he will most likely answer along the lines of "I received Jesus into my heart as my own personal Savior." At a specific point in time, he will claim, Jesus came into his heart. This is the conversion experience. Don't question whether he has had an experience. If the experience is that he came to know Jesus' forgiving love, rejoice with him. If it becomes clear that his joy is in the experience itself and not first and foremost in God's love in Christ, then you have your work cut out for you.

Most Baptists think their experience happened to them because they chose to have Jesus come into them. That is the appeal their pastors make to them. That is what the altar call is all about. Make the request. Make the commitment. Make the promise.

Your Baptist neighbor may be painfully aware of what backsliding is about—going back on your promise and commitment to God. To Baptists, their conversion and continuing life as a believer in Jesus is about what they did and what they continue to do. The emphasis is on them.

As a Lutheran talking to a Baptist, you have a different certainty. Your certainty is not in what you did in claiming Christ as your Savior. Your certainty does not come because of the signs of faith you or others see in your life. Your certainty of salvation comes because of what Jesus did for you and what his Holy Spirit did and does when he "calls, gathers, enlightens, sanctifies, and keeps you"[112] in the one true faith. When your faith flickers, you go back to the light of God's Word. You trust in your God to restore the flame in the same way he created it. You make use of the means of grace (the Word, Baptism, the Lord's Supper) to encourage and inspire and instill faith.

When your Baptist neighbor's faith flickers, he will be inclined to look at himself. He will have to "get back to church." He will wonder if his prayer life is what it should be. He will make greater efforts to bow to God's will and yield his heart to the Spirit. He will spruce up his life so that people once more see his resolve to be a good Christian. He will try to get back the feelings he had right after his conversion experience.

Do you see the difference? Your Baptist friend is not necessarily wrong in what he desires as a Christian. All Christians want to grow in faith and in a sanctified life. The great difference, though, is that what we do as Christians is not what gives us our certainty. Our lives of faith come from our certainty. Our certainty comes from what God does for us. Our certainty does not come from what we do for God. If you understand this difference between you and your Baptist neighbor, you can encourage and help him in a way his church can't and won't.

Baptists love God's grace. They talk about it. They sing John Newton's song "Amazing Grace" and like it just as much as Lutherans do. They nod in agreement when they hear, "It is by grace you have been saved, through faith—and this not from yourselves, it is the gift of God—not by works, so that no one can boast" (Ephesians 2:8,9). But the Baptist understanding of grace can be different from the Lutheran understanding, especially for the majority of Baptists leaning toward Arminian belief (see chapter 2).

Baptists don't hear the words "not by works" in the same way you do. A confessional Lutheran Christian can look a Baptist in the eye and say without any hesitation that the Lutheran church teaches God's grace more fully and completely than the Baptist church does.

This becomes apparent in the Baptists' belief in the sacraments in general. In both Baptism and the Lord's Supper, Baptists believe they are doing something of merit. They are being obedient to what God demands of them. They stress their personal obedience in both. They are baptized as a sign that Jesus came into their lives when they chose to accept Jesus. It is not a way that God brought them into his family and gave them the forgiveness of sins. We hear the Baptist say, "I'm getting baptized, Lord, to show you how much I love you." Baptists don't hear Jesus say to them in Baptism, "I am making you my child. Your sins are all taken away. I promise you heaven. I love you."

They come to the Lord's Supper to remember Jesus' death because he commanded Christians to do this (which is right), but they reject what Christ does for us there, namely, giving us his body and blood for the forgiveness of sins. Again, they partake of the Lord's Supper not to receive something from God but to do something for him. So when the week has been a disappointment and their field of life is covered with broken commandments and shattered resolves, Baptists do not hear Jesus say to them in the Lord's Supper, "It's all right. I forgive you in this Supper you are attending today. I'll take care of the carnage of the week. I already did. Look at the bread and the wine. See my body and blood given and shed for you. Believe my words to you. Understand that you are forgiven and that all can be forgotten. Go home at peace with yourself and me." All the Baptist at the Lord's Supper hears is himself saying, "I have to try harder this next week. I'm here to show you, Lord, that I really mean to be better."

You may hear your friend say about his eight-year-old child, "My child received Christ into his heart. Sunday will be his Baptismal Day." We feel especially sad because our Baptist brothers and sisters have robbed their children of Baptism for the first years of their lives. For your Baptist neighbor, this promise cannot be for his infant children until they are old enough to formally and verbally make their confession and ask

Jesus to become their own personal Savior. We are happy when a Baptist child comes to faith. But what if your neighbors' child dies before he or she is baptized? Here you, as a Lutheran, can help. Let them know that even if their child did not have a "conversion experience," that child heard that Jesus forgave our sins by his death on the cross. That message, we pray, went into the heart of their child and brought him or her into God's family even though their church keeps children from Baptism.

Always go to the Word. Your Baptist friend values the Word. He loves the Bible. Hold him to it. When you have the chance, say, "What do these words say? What is the clearest and easiest way to understand this?" You might even say, "Look, these words of Scripture do say that Baptism saves you. If you asked anyone on the basis of this passage what it is saying, they would have to say it says Baptism saves you. Think of what you are doing then. You are taking words of Scripture that say 'Baptism saves you,' and you are making them say by your teaching 'Baptism does not save you.'"

On a positive note, we can tell of our joy at our little grandchild's baptism. We can refer to our own confidence that Jesus is really present with us in the Lord's Supper. We can be thankful in the presence of our friends at how God's grace frees us and gives us peace and quiet . . . and joy! In our conversation, we can refer to God's Word, particularly as it shows God's grace and power and his faithfulness and put references to this into our conversations.

We can allow our Baptist friends to overhear the gospel in the Word and in the sacraments in our own lives.[113] We can be nonthreatening in this. And because we aren't trying to force anything, but just trying to live it, our neighbor might be tempted to ask us, "How can you be so sure? How can you be so relaxed? How can you be so happy?"

With God's help, give all your words and how you live a high volume of God's grace in Christ so that Baptists and all others may hear their Savior talking. If your discussions with your Baptist friend revolve around God's grace, your friend will see you as a brother or sister in Christ. Your friend will respect you. The Lord may open the door for you to talk about the complete, 100 percent hope you have in what your Savior has done for you. Your friend may realize that your Lutheran church does indeed teach grace better than the Baptist church. Will you be able to lead your Baptist friend into your church? Perhaps you will, when your friend is comforted as you speak about God's kindness and grace in contrast to his church that may be focusing on God's law and obedience, obedience, and more obedience.

Wouldn't it be a wonderful thing if our Baptist neighbors would overhear new and comforting things about Jesus through what we say and do? That's the very reason for this book and the Lord's encouragement to "always be prepared to give an answer to everyone who asks you to give the reason for the hope that you have" (1 Peter 3:15).

ADDENDUM

This addendum contains sections from *The 1677/89 London Baptist Confession of Faith*. Some have been included because they are referred to in this book; others, because they are of general interest. Note the strong Calvinistic emphasis throughout. We included the appendix, which contains the early Baptists' complete argument against infant Baptism. Many, perhaps most, of these arguments are still used.

In using this document to evaluate present-day Baptist teachings, remember that today most are Arminian in flavor, promoting some form of decision theology. An Internet search will help you locate the full text of this confession in both the Old English, as reproduced here, and in modern English (which we were unable to use for copyright reasons). You will also find more recent Baptist confessions that reflect current Arminian theology.

The 1677/89 London Baptist Confession of Faith
Thirty-Two Articles of Christian Faith
and Practice with Scripture Proofs

Adopted by the Ministers and Messengers
of the General Assembly

Which Met in London in 1689

To the
Judicious* and *Impartial
Reader

Courteous Reader,
It is now many years since divers of us (with other sober

Christians then living and walking in the way of the Lord that we professe) did conceive our selves to be under a necessity of Publishing a *Confession of our Faith,* for the information, and satisfaction of those, that did not thoroughly understand what our principles were, or had entertained prejudices against our Profession, by reason of the strange representation of them, by some men of note, who had taken very wrong measures, and accordingly led others into misapprehensions, of us, and them: and this was first put forth about the year, 1643. in the name of seven Congregations then gathered in *London;* since which time, diverse impressions thereof have been dispersed abroad, and our end proposed, in good measure answered, inasmuch as many (and some of those men eminent, both for piety and learning) were thereby satisfied, that we were no way guilty of those Heterodoxies and fundamental errors, which had too frequently been charged upon us without ground, or occasion given on our part. And forasmuch, as that *Confession* is not now commonly to be had; and also that many others have since embraced the same truth which is owned therein; it was judged necessary by us to joyn together in giving a testimony to the world; of our firm adhering to those wholesome Principles, by the publication of this which is now in your hand.

And forasmuch as our method, and manner of expressing our sentiments, in this, doth vary from the former (although the substance of the matter is the same) we shall freely impart to you the reason and occasion thereof. One thing that greatly prevailed with us to undertake this work, was (not only to give a full account of our selves, to those Christians that differ from us about the subject of Baptism, but also) the profit that might from thence arise, unto those that have any account of our labors, in their instruction, and establishment in the great truths of the Gospel; in the clear understanding, and steady belief of which, our comfortable walking with God, and fruitfulness before him, in all our ways, is most neerly concerned; and therefore we did conclude it necessary to expresse our selves the more fully, and distinctly; and also to fix on such a method as might be most comprehensive of those things which we designed to explain our sense, and belief of; and finding no defect, in this regard, in that fixed on by the assembly, and after them by those of the Congregational way, we did readily conclude it best to retain the same *order* in our present confession: and also, when we observed that those last mentioned, did in their confession (for reasons which seemed of weight both to themselves and others) choose not only to express their mind in words concurrent with the former in sense, concerning all those articles wherein they were agreed, but also for the most part without any variation of the terms we did in like manner conclude it best to follow their example in making use of the very same words with them both, in these articles (which are very many) wherein our faith and doctrine is the same with theirs, and this we did, the more abundantly, to manifest our consent with both, in all the fundamental articles of the Christian Religion, as also with many others, whose orthodox confessions have been published to the world; on behalf of the Protestants in divers Nations and Cities: and also to convince all, that we have no itch to clogge Religion with new words, but do readily acquiesce in that form of sound words, which hath been, in consent with the holy Scriptures, used by others before us; hereby declaring before God, Angels, & Men, our hearty agreement with them, in that wholesome Protestant Doctrine, which with so clear evidence of Scriptures they have asserted: some things indeed, are in some places added, some terms omitted, and some few changed, but these alterations are of that nature, as that we need not doubt, any charge or suspition of unsoundness in the faith, from any of our brethren upon the account of them.

In those things wherein we differ from others, we have exprest our selves with all candor and plainness that none might entertain jealousie of ought secretly lodged in our breasts, that we would not the world should be acquainted with; yet we hope we have also observed those rules of modesty, and humility, as will render our freedom in this respect inoffensive, even to those whose sentiments are different from ours.

We have also taken care to affix texts of Scripture, in the margin for the confirmation of each article in our confession; in which work we have studiously indeavoured to select such as are most clear and pertinent, for the proof of what is asserted by us: and our earnest desire is, that all into whose hands this may come, would follow that (never enough commended) example of the noble *Bereans,* who searched the Scriptures daily, that they might find out whether the things preached to them were so or not. [These passages have been removed in this book for the sake of brevity. They can be found on the Web site.]

There is one thing more which we sincerely professe, and earnestly desire credence in, *viz.* That contention is most remote from our design in all that we have done in this matter: and we hope the liberty of an ingenuous unfolding our principles, and opening our hearts unto our Brethren, with the Scripture grounds on which our faith and practise leanes, will by none of them be either denied to us, or taken ill from us. Our whole design is accomplished, if we may obtain that Justice, as to be measured in our principles, and practise, and the judgement of both by others, according to what we have now published; which the Lord (whose eyes are as a flame of fire) knoweth to be the doctrine, which with our hearts we must firmly believe, and sincerely indeavour to conform our lives to. And oh that other contentions being laid asleep, the only care and contention of all upon whom the name of our blessed Redeemer is called, might for the future be, to walk humbly with their God, and in the exercise of all Love and Meekness towards each other, to perfect holyness in the fear of the Lord, each one indeavouring to have his conversation such as becometh the Gospel; and also suitable to his place and capacity vigorously to promote in others the practice of true Religion and undefiled in the sight of God and our Father. And that in this backsliding day, we might not spend our breath in fruitless complaints of the evils of others; but may every one begin at home, to reform in the first place our own hearts, and wayes; and then to quicken all that we may have influence upon, to the same work; that if the will of God were so, none might deceive themselves, by resting in, and trusting to, a form of Godliness, without the power of it, and inward experience of the efficacy of those truths that are professed by them.

And verily there is one spring and cause of the decay of Religion in our day, which we cannot but touch upon, and earnestly urge a redresse of; and that is the neglect of the worship of God in Families, by those to whom the charge and conduct of them is committed. May not the grosse ignorance, and instability of many; with the prophaneness of others, be justly charged upon their Parents and Masters; who have not trained them up in the way wherein they ought to walk when they were young? but have neglected those frequent and solemn commands which the Lord hath laid upon them so to catechize, and instruct them, that their tender years might be seasoned with the knowledge of the truth of God as revealed in the Scriptures; and also by their own omission of Prayer, and other duties of Religion in their families, together with the ill example of their loose conversation, have inured them first to a neglect, and then contempt of all Piety and Religion? we know this will not excuse the blindness, or wickedness of any; but certainly it will fall heavy upon those that have thus been the occasion thereof; they indeed dye in their sins; but will not their blood be required of those under whose care they were, who yet permitted them to go on without *warning,* yea led them into the paths of destruction? and will not the diligence of Christians with respect to the discharge of these duties, in ages past, rise up in judgment against, and condemn many of those who would be esteemed such now?

We shall conclude with our earnest prayer, that the God of all grace, will pour out those measures of his holy Spirit upon us, that the profession of truth may be accompanyed with the sound belief, and diligent practise of it by us; that his name may in all things be glorified, through Jesus Christ our Lord, *Amen.*

Chapter 1: Of the Holy Scriptures

Chapter 2: Of God and of the Holy Trinity

Chapter 3: Of God's Decree

[Proof passages for lettered items can be found online: search Creeds of Christendom, Baptist, "The 1677/89 BCF Assistant".]

1. God hath *(a) Decreed* in himself from all Eternity, by the most wise and holy Councel of his own will, freely and unchangeably, all things whatsoever comes to passe; yet so as thereby is God neither the author of sin, *(b)* nor hath fellowship with any therein, nor is violence offered to the will of the Creature, nor yet is the liberty, or contingency of second causes taken away, but rather *(c)* established, in which appears his wisdom in disposing all things, and power, and faithfulness *(d)* in accomplishing his *Decree.*
2. Although God knoweth whatsoever may, or can come to passe upon all *(e)* supposed conditions; yet hath he not *Decreed* anything, *(f)* because he foresaw it as future, or as that which would come to pass upon such conditions.
3. By the *decree* of God for the manifestation of his glory *(g)* some men and Angels, are predestinated, or fore-ordained to Eternal Life, through Jesus Christ to the *(h)* praise of his glorious grace; others being left to act in their sin to their *(i)* just condemnation, to the praise of his glorious justice.
4. These Angels and Men thus predestinated, and fore-ordained, are particularly, and unchangeably designed; and their *(k)* number so certain, and definite, that it cannot be either increased, or diminished.
5. Those of mankind *(l)* that are predestinated to life, God

before the foundation of the world was laid, according to his eternal and immutable purpose, and the secret Councel and good pleasure of his will, hath chosen in Christ unto everlasting glory, out of his meer free grace and love; *(m)* without any other thing in the creature as a condition or cause moving him thereunto.
6. As God hath appointed the Elect unto glory, so he hath by the eternal and most free purpose of his will, fore-ordained *(o)* all the means thereunto, wherefore they who are elected, being fallen in Adam, *(p)* are redeemed by Christ, are effectually *(q)* called unto faith in Christ, by his spirit working in due season, are justifyed, adopted, sanctified, and kept by his power through faith *(r)* unto salvation; neither are any other redeemed by Christ, or effectually called, justified, adopted, sanctified, and saved, but the Elect *(s)* only.
7. The Doctrine of this high mystery of predestination, is to be handled with special prudence, and care; that men attending the will of God revealed in his word, and yielding obedience thereunto, may from the certainty of their effectual vocation, be assured of their *(t)* eternal election; so shall this doctrine afford matter *(u)* of praise, reverence, and admiration of God, and *(x)* of humility, diligence, and abundant *(y)* consolation, to all that sincerely obey the Gospel.

Chapter 4: Of Creation

Chapter 5: Of Divine Providence

1. God the good *Creator* of all things, in *his* infinite power, and wisdom, doth *(a)* uphold, direct, dispose, and govern all Creatures, and things, from the greatest even to the *(b)* least, by his most wise and holy providence, to the end for the which they were *Created;* according unto his infallible foreknowledge, and the free and immutable Councel of *his (c)* own will; to the praise of the glory of his wisdom, power, justice, infinite goodness and mercy.

2. Although in relation to the foreknowledge and *Decree* of *God,* the first cause, all things come to pass *(d)* immutably and infallibly; so that there is not any thing, befalls any *(e)* by chance, or without *his Providence;* yet by the same *Providence* he ordereth them to fall out, according to the nature of second causes, either *(f)* necessarily, freely, or contingently.
3. God in his ordinary *Providence (g)* maketh use of means; yet is free *(h)* to work, without, *(i)* above, and *(k)* against them at his pleasure.
4. The Almighty power, unsearchable wisdom, and *infinite* goodness of *God,* so far manifest themselves in *his Providence,* that *his* determinate Councel *(l)* extendeth it self even to the first fall, and all other sinful actions both of Angels, and Men; (and that not by a bare permission) which also he most wisely and powerfully *(m)* boundeth, and otherwise ordereth, and governeth, in a manifold dispensation to his most holy *(n)* ends: yet so, as the sinfulness of their acts proceedeth only from the Creatures, and not from *God;* who being most holy and righteous, neither is nor can be, the author or *(o)* approver of sin.
5. The most wise, righteous, and gracious *God,* doth oftentimes, leave for a season his own children to manifold temptations, and the corruptions of their own heart, to chastise them for their former sins, or to discover unto them the hidden strength of corruption, and deceitfulness of their hearts, *(p)* that they may be humbled; and to raise them to a more close, and constant dependence for their support, upon himself; and to make them more watchful against all future occasions of sin, and for other just and holy ends.

So that whatsoever befalls any of his elect is by his appointment, for his glory, *(q)* and their good.
6. As for those wicked and ungodly men, whom God as a righteous judge, for former sin doth *(r)* blind and harden;

from them he not only withholdeth his *(s)* Grace, whereby they might have been inlightned in their understanding, and wrought upon in their hearts: But sometimes also withdraweth *(t)* the gifts which they had, and exposeth them to such *(u)* objects as their *corruptions* makes occasion of sin; and withall *(x)* gives them over to their own lusts, the temptations of the world, and the power of Satan, whereby it comes to pass, that they *(y)* harden themselves, even under those means which God useth for the softning of others.

7. As the *Providence* of *God* doth in general reach to all *Creatures,* so after a most special manner it taketh care of his *(z)* Church, and disposeth of all things to the good thereof.

Chapter 6: Of the Fall of Man, of Sin, and of the Punishment Thereof

1. Although *God created Man* upright, and perfect, and gave him a righteous law, which had been unto life had he kept it, *(a)* and threatned death upon the breach thereof; yet he did not long abide in this honour; *(b)* Satan using the subtilty of the serpent to seduce *Eve,* then by her seducing *Adam,* who without any compulsion, did wilfully transgress the Law of their *Creation,* and the command given unto them, in eating the forbidden fruit; which *God* was pleased according to *his* wise and holy *Councel* to permit, having purposed to order it, to *his* own glory.

2. Our first *Parents* by this *Sin,* fell from their *(c)* original righteousness and communion with *God,* and we in them, whereby death came upon all; *(d)* all becoming dead in *Sin,* and wholly defiled, *(e)* in all the faculties, and parts, of soul, and body.

3. They being the *(f)* root, and by *Gods* appointment, standing in the room, and stead of all mankind; the guilt of the *Sin* was imputed, and *corrupted* nature conveyed, to all their posterity descending from them by ordinary

generation, being now *(g)* conceived in *Sin,* and by nature children *(h)* of wrath, the servants of *Sin,* the subjects *(i)* of death and all other miseries, spiritual, temporal and eternal, unless the *Lord Jesus (k)* set them free.
4. From this original *corruption,* whereby we are *(l)* utterly indisposed, disabled, and made opposite to all good, and wholly inclined to all evil, do *(m)* proceed all actual transgressions.
5. The *corruption* of nature, during this Life, doth *(n)* remain in those that are regenerated: and although it be through *Christ* pardoned, and mortified, yet both it self, and the first motions thereof, are truely and properly *(o)* Sin.

Chapter 7: Of God's Covenant
1. The distance between *God* and the *Creature* is so great, that although reasonable *Creatures* do owe obedience unto him as their *Creator,* yet they could never have attained the reward of Life, but by some *(a)* voluntary condescension on *Gods part,* which he hath been pleased to express, by way of *Covenant.*
2. Moreover *Man* having brought himself *(b)* under the *curse* of the Law by his fall, it pleased the *Lord* to make a *Covenant* of *Grace* wherein he freely offereth unto *Sinners, (c)* Life and Salvation by *Jesus Christ,* requiring of them Faith in him, that they may be saved; and *(d)* promising to give unto all those that are ordained unto eternal Life, his holy *Spirit,* to make them willing, and able to believe.
3. This *Covenant* is revealed in the Gospel; first of all to *Adam* in the promise of Salvation by the *(e)* seed of the woman, and afterwards by farther steps, until the full *(f)* discovery thereof was compleated in the new Testament; and it is founded in that (*) Eternal *Covenant* transaction, that was between the *Father* and the *Son,* about the Redemption of the *Elect;* and it is alone by the Grace of this *Covenant,* that all of the posterity of fallen *Adam,*

that ever were *(g)* saved, did obtain life and a blessed immortality; *Man* being now utterly uncapable of acceptance with *God* upon those terms, on which *Adam* stood in his state of innocency.

Chapter 8: Of Christ the Mediator

1. It pleased *God* in his eternal purpose, to chuse and ordain the *Lord Jesus* his only begotten *Son,* according to the *Covenant* made between them both, *(a)* to be the *Mediator* between *God* and *Man;* the *(b)* Prophet, *(c)* Priest and *(d)* King; Head and Saviour of his Church, the heir of all things, and judge of the world: Unto whom he did from all Eternity *(e)* give a people to be his seed, and to be by him in time redeemed, called, justified, sanctified, and glorified.

2. The *Son* of *God,* the second Person in the *Holy Trinity,* being very and eternal *God,* the brightness of the Fathers glory, of one substance and equal with *him:* who made the World, who upholdeth and governeth all things he hath made: did when the fullness of time was come take unto him *(f)* mans nature, with all the Essential properties, and common infirmities thereof, *(g)* yet without sin: being conceived by the *Holy Spirit* in the *Womb* of the *Virgin Mary,* the *Holy Spirit* coming down upon her, and the power of the most *High* overshadowing her, *(h)* and so was made of a *Woman,* of the Tribe of *Judah,* of the Seed of *Abraham,* and *David* according to the *Scriptures:* So that two whole, perfect, and distinct natures, were inseparably joined together in one *Person:* without *conversion, composition,* or *confusion:* which *Person* is very *God,* and very *Man;* yet one *(i) Christ,* the only *Mediator* between *God* and *Man.*

3. The *Lord Jesus* in his humane nature thus united to the divine, in the Person of the *Son,* was sanctified, & anointed *(k)* with the *Holy Spirit,* above measure; having in him *(l)* all the treasures of wisdom and knowledge; in

whom it pleased the *Father* that *(m)* all fullness should dwell: To the end that being *(n)* holy, harmless, undefiled, and full *(o)* of *Grace,* and *Truth,* he might be throughly furnished to execute the office of a *Mediator,* and *(p) Surety;* which office he took not upon himself, but was thereunto *(q)* called by his *Father;* who also put *(r)* all power and judgement in his hand, and gave him Commandment to execute the same.

4. This office the *Lord Jesus* did most *(s)* willingly undertake, which that he might discharge he was made under the Law, *(t)* and did perfectly fulfill it, and underwent the *(u)* punishment due to us, which we should have born and suffered, being made *(x) Sin* and a *Curse* for us: enduring most grievous sorrows *(y)* in his Soul; and most painful sufferings in his body; was crucified, and died, and remained in the state of the dead; yet saw no *(z) corruption:* on the (a) third day he arose from the dead, with the same (b) body in which he suffered; with which he also (c) ascended into heaven: and there sitteth at the right hand of *his Father,* (d) making intercession; and shall (e) return to judge *Men* and *Angels,* at the end of the World.

5. The *Lord Jesus* by his perfect obedience and sacrifice of himself, which he through the Eternal *Spirit* once offered up unto *God,* (f) hath fully satisfied the Justice of *God,* procured reconciliation, and purchased an Everlasting inheritance in the Kingdom of Heaven, (g) for all those whom the *Father* hath given unto him.

6. Although the price of Redemption was not actually paid by *Christ,* till after his *Incarnation,* (*) yet the vertue, efficacy, and benefit thereof were communicated to the Elect in all ages successively, from the beginning of the World, in and by those Promises, Types, and Sacrifices, wherein he was revealed, and signified to be the Seed of the *Woman,* which should bruise the Serpents head; (h) and the Lamb slain from the foundation of the World: (i) Being *the same yesterday, and today, and for ever.*

7. Christ in the work of *Mediation* acteth according to both natures, by each nature doing that which is proper to it self; yet by reason of the Unity of the Person, that which is proper to one nature, is sometimes in *Scripture* attributed to the Person (k) denominated by the other nature.
8. To all those for whom Christ hath obtained eternal redemption, he doth certainly, and effectually (l) apply, and communicate the same; making intercession for them, uniting them to himself by his spirit, (m) revealing unto them, in and by the word, the mystery of salvation; perswading them to believe, and obey; (n) governing their hearts by his word and spirit, and (o) overcoming all their enemies by his Almighty power, and wisdom; in such manner, and wayes as are most consonant to his wonderful, and (p) unsearchable dispensation; and all of free, and absolute Grace, without any condition foreseen in them, to procure it.
9. This office of Mediator between God and Man, is proper (q) only to Christ, who is the Prophet, Priest, and King of the Church of God; and may not be either in whole, or any part thereof transfer'd from him to any other.
10. This number and order of Offices is necessary; for in respect of our (r) ignorance, we stand in need of his prophetical Office; and in respect of our alienation from God, (s) and imperfection of the best of our services, we need his Priestly office, to reconcile us, and present us acceptable unto God: and in respect o our averseness, and utter inability to return to God, and for our rescue, and security from our spiritual adversaries, we need his Kingly office, (t) to convince, subdue, draw, uphold, deliver, and preserve us to his Heavenly Kingdome.

Chapter 9: Of Free Will

1. God hath indued the Will of Man, with that natural liberty, and power of acting upon choice; that it is *(a)* neither forced, nor by any necessity of nature determined to do good or evil.

2. Man by his fall into a state of sin hath wholly lost *(d)* all ability of Will, to any spiritual good accompanying salvation; so as a natural man, being altogether averse from that good, *(e)* and dead in *Sin,* is not able, by his own strength, to *(f)* convert himself; or to prepare himself thereunto.
3. Man by his fall into a state of sin hath wholly lost all ability of Will, to any spiritual good accompanying salvation; so as a Sin, is not able, by his own strength, to convert himself; or to prepare himself thereunto.
4. When God converts a sinner, and translates him into the state of Grace *(g)* he freeth him from his natural bondage under sin, and by his grace alone, enables him *(h)* freely to will, and to do that which is spiritually good; yet so as that by reason of his *(i)* remaining corruptions he doth not perfectly nor only will that which is good; but doth also will that which is evil.
5. The Will of Man is made *(k)* perfectly, and immutably free to good alone, in the state of Glory only.

Chapter 10: Of Effectual Calling

1. Those whom God hath predestinated unto Life, he is pleased in his appointed, and accepted time, *(a)* effectually to call by his word, and Spirit, out of that state of sin, and death, in which they are by nature, to grace and Salvation *(b)* by Jesus Christ; inlightning their minds, spiritually, and savingly to *(c)* understand the things of God; taking away their *(d)* heart of stone, and giving unto them an heart of flesh; renewing their wills, and by his Almighty power determining them *(e)* to that which is good, and effectually drawing them to Jesus Christ; yet so as they come *(f)* most freely, being made willing by his Grace.
2. This Effectual Call is of God's free, and special grace alone, *(g)* not from any thing at all foreseen in man, nor from any power, or agency in the Creature, coworking

with his special Grace, *(h)* the Creature being wholly passive therein, being dead in sins and trespasses, until being quickned & renewed by the holy Spirit, he is thereby enabled to answer this call, and to embrace the Grace offered and conveyed in it; and that by no less *(i)* power, then that which raised up Christ from the dead.
3. Elect Infants dying in infancy, are *(k)* regenerated and saved by Christ through the Spirit; who worketh when, and where, and *(l)* how he pleaseth: so also are all other elect persons, who are uncapable of being outwardly called by the Ministry of the Word.
4. Others not elected, although they may be called by the Ministry of the word, *(m)* and may have some common operations of the Spirit, yet not being effectually drawn by the Father, they neither will, nor can truly *(n)* come to Christ; and therefore cannot be saved: much less can men that receive not the Christian Religion *(o)* be saved; be they never so diligent to frame their lives according to the light of nature, and the Law of that Religion they do profess.

Chapter 11: Of Justification

1. Those whom God Effectually calleth, he also freely *(a)* justifieth, not by infusing Righteousness into them, but by *(b)* pardoning their sins, and by accounting, and accepting their Persons as *(c)* Righteous; not for any thing wrought in them, or done by them, but for Christ's sake alone, not by imputing faith it self, the act of believing, or any other *(d)* evangelical obedience to them, as their Righteousness; but by imputing Christs active obedience unto the whole Law, and passive obedience in his death, for their whole and sole Righteousness, they *(e)* receiving, and resting on him, and his Righteousness, by Faith; which faith they have not of themselves, it is the gift of *God*.
2. Faith thus receiving and resting on Christ, and his Righteousness, is the *(f)* alone instrument of Justification:

yet it is not alone in the person justified, but is ever accompanied with all other saving Graces, and is no dead faith, *(g)* but worketh by love.
3. Christ by his obedience, and death, did fully discharge the debt of all those that are justified; and did by the sacrifice of himself, in the blood of his cross, undergoing in their stead, the penalty due unto them: make a proper, real and full satisfaction *(h)* to *Gods* justice in their behalf: yet in as much as he was given by the Father for them, and his Obedience and Satisfaction accepted in their stead, and both *(i)* freely, not for any thing in them; their Justification is only of Free Grace, that both the exact justice and rich Grace of *God,* might be *(k)* glorified in the Justification of sinners.
4. God did from all eternity decree to *(l)* justifie all the Elect, and Christ did in the fulness of time die for their sins, and rise *(m)* again for their Justification; Nevertheless they are not justified personally, untill the *Holy Spirit,* doth in due time *(n)* actually apply *Christ* unto them.
5. God doth continue to *(o)* Forgive the sins of those that are justified, and although they can never fall from the state of *(p)* justification; yet they may by their sins fall under *Gods (q)* Fatherly displeasure; and in that condition, they have not usually the light of his Countenance restored unto them, untill they *(r)* humble themselves, confess their sins, beg pardon, and renew their faith, and repentance.
6. The Justification of Believers under the Old Testament was in all these respects, *(s)* one and the same with the justification of Believers under the New Testament.

Chapter 12: Of Adoption

1. All those that are justified, *God* vouchsafed, in, and for the sake of his only *Son Jesus Christ,* to make partakers of the Grace *(a)* of *Adoption;* by which they are taken into the number, and enjoy the Liberties, and *(b)*

Priveledges of Children of *God;* have his *(c)* name put upon them, *(d)* receive the *Spirit* of *Adoption,* *(e)* have access to the throne of Grace with boldness, are enabled to cry *Abba, Father,* are *(f)* pitied, *(g)* protected, *(i)* provided for, and *(k)* chastned by him, as by a Father; yet never *(l)* cast off; but sealed *(m)* to the day of Redemption, and inherit the promises, *(n)* as heirs, of everlasting Salvation.

Chapter 13: Of Sanctification

1. They who are united to *Christ,* Effectually called, and regenerated, having a new heart, and a new *Spirit created* in them, through the vertue of *Christ's* death, and Resurrection; are also *(a)* farther sanctified, really, and personally, through the same vertue, *(b)* by his word and *Spirit* dwelling in them; *(c)* the dominion of the whole body of sin is destroyed, *(d)* and the several lusts thereof, are more and more weakned, and mortified; and they more and more quickened, and *(e)* strengthned in all saving graces, to the *(f)* practice of all true holyness, without which no man shall see the Lord.
2. This Sanctification is *(g)* throughout, in the whole man, yet imperfect *(h)* in this life; there abideth still some remnants of *corruption* in every part, whence ariseth a *(i)* continual, and irreconcilable war; the Flesh lusting against the Spirit, and the Spirit against the Flesh.
3. In which war, although the remaining corruption for a time may much *(k)* prevail; yet through the continual supply of strength from the sanctifying *Spirit* of *Christ* the *(l)* regenerate part doth overcome; and so the Saints grow in Grace, perfecting holiness in the fear of God, *(m)* pressing after an heavenly life, in Evangelical Obedience to all the commands which *Christ* as *Head* and *King,* in his *Word* hath prescribed to them.

Chapter 14: Of Saving Faith

1. The Grace of *Faith*, whereby the Elect are enabled to believe to the saving of their souls, is the work of the *Spirit* of *Christ (a)* in their hearts; and is ordinarily wrought by the Ministry of the *(b)* Word; by which also, and by the administration of *Baptisme,* and the *Lords Supper, Prayer* and other *Means* appointed of *God,* it is increased, *(c)* and strengthned.

2. By this *Faith,* a Christian believeth to be true, (*) whatsoever is revealed in the *Word,* for the Authority of *God* himself; and also apprehendeth an excellency therein, *(d)* above all other *Writings;* and all things in the *world*: as it bears forth the Glory of *God* in his *Attributes,* the excellency of *Christ* in his Nature and Offices; and the Power and Fullness of the *Holy Spirit* in his Workings, and Operations; and so is enabled to *(e)* cast his Soul upon the truth thus believed; and also acteth differently, upon that which each particular, passage thereof containeth; yielding obedience to the *(f)* commands, trembling at the *(g)* threatnings, and embracing the *(h)* promises of *God,* for this life, and that which is to come: But the principal acts of Saving Faith, have immediate relation to *Christ,* accepting, receiving, and resting upon *(i)* him alone, for Justification, Sanctification, and Eternal Life, by vertue of the Covenant of Grace.

3. This *Faith* although it be different in degrees, and may be weak, *(k)* or strong; yet it is in the least degree of it, different in the kind, or nature of it (as is all other saving Grace) from the Faith, *(l)* and common grace of temporary believers; and therefore though it may be many times assailed, and weakned; yet it gets *(m)* the victory; growing up in many, to the attainment of a full *(n)* assurance through *Christ,* who is both the Author *(o)* and finisher of our *Faith*.

Chapter 15: Of Repentance Unto Life and Salvation

1. Such of the Elect as are converted at riper years, having *(a)* sometimes lived in the state of nature, and therein served divers lusts and pleasures, *God* in their *Effectual Calling* giveth them Repentance unto Life.
2. Whereas there is none that doth good, and sinneth *(b)* not; and the best of men may through the power, and deceitfulness of their corruption dwelling in them, with the prevalency of temptation, fall into great sins, and provocations; God hath in the Covenant of Grace, mercifully provided that Believers so sinning, and falling, *(c)* be renewed through Repentance unto Salvation.
3. This saving Repentance is an *(d)* evangelical Grace, whereby a person being by the *Holy Spirit* made sensible of the manifold evils of his sin, doth, by Faith in Christ, humble himself for it, with godly sorrow, detestation of it, and self abhorrency; *(e)* praying for pardon, and strength of grace, with a purpose and endeavour by supplies of the *Spirit,* to *(f)* walk before God unto all well pleasing in all things.
4. As Repentance is to be continued through the whole course of our lives, upon the account of the body of death, and the motions thereof; so it is every mans duty, to repent of his *(g)* particular known sins, particularly.
5. Such is the provision which God hath made through Christ in the Covenant of Grace, for the preservation of Believers unto Salvation, that although there is no sin so small, but it deserves *(h)* damnation; yet there is no sin so great, that it shall bring damnation on them that *(i)* repent; which makes the constant preaching of Repentance necessary.

Chapter 16: Of Good Works

Chapter 17: Of the Perseverance of the Saints

1. Those whom God hath accepted in the beloved, effectually called and Sanctified by his *Spirit,* and given

the precious faith of his Elect unto, can neither totally nor finally fall from the state of grace; *(a)* but shall certainly persevere therein to the end and be eternally saved, seeing the gifts and callings of God are without Repentance, (whence he still begets and nourisheth in them Faith, Repentance, Love, Joy, Hope, and all the graces of the Spirit unto immortality) and though many storms and floods arise and beat against them, yet they shall never be able to take them off that foundation and rock which by faith they are fastned upon: notwithstanding through unbelief and the temptations of Satan the sensible sight of the light and love of God, may for a time be clouded, and obscured from *(b)* them, yet he is still the same *(c)* and they shall be sure to be kept by the power of God unto Salvation, where they shall enjoy their purchased possession, they being engraven upon the palm of his hands, and their names having been written in the book of life from all Eternity.
2. This perseverance of the Saints depends not upon their own free will; but upon the immutability of the decree of *(d)* Election flowing from the free and unchangeable love of God the Father; upon the efficacy of the merit and intercession of Jesus Christ *(e)* and Union with him, the *(f)* oath of God, the abiding of his Spirit & the *(g)* seed of God within them, and the nature of the *(h)* Covenant of Grace from all which ariseth also the certainty and infallibility thereof.
3. And though they may through the temptation of Satan and of the world, the prevalency of corruption remaining in them, and the neglect of means of their preservation fall into grievous *(i)* sins, and for a time continue therein; whereby they incur *(k)* Gods displeasure, and grieve his holy Spirit, come to have their graces and *(l)* comforts impaired have their hearts hardened, and their Consciences wounded, *(m)* hurt, and scandalize others, and bring temporal judgements *(n)* upon themselves: yet

they shall renew their *(o)* repentance and be preserved through faith in Christ Jesus to the end.

Chapter 18: Of the Assurance of Grace and Salvation

1. Although temporary Believers, and other unregenerate men, may vainly deceive themselves with false hopes, and carnal presumptions, of being in the favour of God, and state of salvation, *(a)* which hope of theirs shall perish; yet such as truely believe in the Lord Jesus, and love him in sincerity, endeavouring to walk in all good Conscience before him, may in this life be certainly assured *(b)* that they are in the state of Grace; and may rejoyce in the hope of the glory of God which hope shall never make them *(c)* ashamed.

2. This certainty is not a bare conjectural, and probable perswasion, grounded upon *(d)* a fallible hope; but an infallible assurance of faith founded on the Blood and Righteousness of Christ *(e)* revealed in the Gospel; and also upon the inward *(f)* evidence of those graces of the Spirit unto which promises are made, and on the testimony of the *(g)* Spirit of adoption, witnessing with our Spirits that we are the children of God; and as a fruit thereof keeping the heart both *(h)* humble and holy.

3. This infallible assurance doth not so belong to the essence of faith, but that a true Believer, may wait long and conflict with many difficulties before he be *(i)* partaker of it; yet being enabled by the Spirit to know the things which are freely given him of God, he may without extraordinary revelation in the right use of means *(k)* attain thereunto: and therefore it is the duty of every one, to give all diligence to make their Calling and Election sure, that thereby his heart may be enlarged in peace and joy in the holy Spirit, in love and thankfulness to God, and in strength and chearfulness in the duties of obedience, the proper *(l)* fruits of this Assurance; so far is it *(m)* from inclining men to looseness.

4. True Believers may have the assurance of their Salvation divers ways shaken, diminished, and intermitted; as *(n)* by negligence in preserving of it, by *(o)* falling into some special *Sin,* which woundeth the Conscience, and grieveth the *Spirit,* by some sudden or *(p)* vehement temptation, by Gods withdrawing the *(q)* light of his countenance and suffering even such as fear him to walk in darkness and to have no light; yet are they never destitute of the *(r)* seed of God, and Life *(s)* of Faith, that Love of Christ, and the brethren, that sincerity of Heart, and Conscience of duty, out of which by the operation of the Spirit, this Assurance may in due time be *(t)* revived: and by the which in the mean time they are *(u)* preserved from utter despair.

Chapter 19: Of the Law of God

Chapter 20: Of the Gospel, and of the Extent of the Grace Thereof

1. The Covenant of Works being broken by Sin, and made unprofitable unto Life; God was pleased to give forth the promise of *Christ, (a)* the Seed of the Woman, as the means of calling the Elect, and begetting in them Faith and Repentance; in this Promise, the *(b)* Gospel, as to the substance of it, was revealed, and therein Effectual, for the Conversion and Salvation of Sinners.
2. This Promise of *Christ,* and Salvation by him, is revealed only by *(c)* the Word of God; neither do the Works of Creation, or Providence, with the light of Nature, *(d)* make discovery of *Christ,* or of *Grace* by him; so much as in a general, or obscure way; much less that men destitute of the Revelation of him by the Promise, or Gospel; *(e)* should be enabled thereby, to attain saving Faith, or Repentance.
3. The Revelation of the Gospel unto Sinners, made in divers times, and by sundry parts; with the addition of Promises, and Precepts for the Obedience required

therein, as to the Nations, and Persons, to whom it is granted, is meerly of the *(f)* Soveraign Will and good Pleasure of God; not being annexed by vertue of any Promise, to the due improvement of mens natural abilities, by vertue of Common light received, without it; which none ever did *(g)* make, or can so do: And therefore in all Ages the preaching of the Gospel hath been granted unto persons and Nations, as to the extent, or streightning of it, in great variety, according to the Councel of the Will of God.

4. Although the Gospel be the only outward means, of revealing *Christ,* and saving Grace; and is, as such, abundantly sufficient thereunto; yet that men who are dead in Trespasses, may be born again, Quickned or Regenerated; there is moreover necessary, an effectual, insuperable *(h)* work of the Holy *Spirit,* upon the whole Soul, for the producing in them a new spiritual Life; without which no other means will effect *(i)* their Conversion unto God.

Chapter 21: Of Christian Liberty and Liberty of Conscience

Chapter 22: Of Religious Worship and the Sabbath Day

1. The light of Nature shews that there is a God, who hath Lordship, and Soveraigntye over all; is just, good, and doth good unto all; and is therefore to be feared, loved, praised, called upon, trusted in, and served, with all the Heart, and all the Soul, *(a)* and with all the Might. But the acceptable way of Worshipping the true God, is *(b)* instituted by himself; and so limited by his own revealed will, that he may not be Worshipped according to the imaginations, and devices of Men, or the suggestions of Satan, under any visible representations, or *(c)* any other way, not prescribed in the Holy Scriptures.

2. *Religious Worship* is to be given to *God* the *Father, Son,* and *Holy Spirit,* and to him *(d)* alone; not to *Angels, Saints,* or any other *(e) Creatures;* and since the fall, not without a *(f) Mediator,* nor in the *Mediation* of any other but *(g)* Christ alone.
3. Prayer with thanksgiving, being one special part of natural worship, is by *God* required of *(h)* all men. But that it may be accepted, it is to be made in the *(i)* Name of the Son, by the help *(k)* of the Spirit, according to *(l)* his Will; with understanding, reverence, humility, fervency, faith, love, and perseverance; and when with others, in a *(m)* known tongue.
4. Prayer is to be made for things lawful, and for all sorts of men living, *(n)* or that shall live hereafter; but not *(o)* for the dead, nor for those of whom it may be known that they have sinned *(p)* the sin unto death.
5. The *(q)* reading of the Scriptures, Preaching, and *(r)* hearing the word of God, teaching and admonishing one another in Psalms, Hymns and Spiritual songs, singing with grace in our Hearts to *(s)* the Lord; as also the Administration *(t)* of Baptism, and *(u)* the Lords Supper are all parts of Religious worship of *God,* to be performed in obedience to him, with understanding, faith, reverence, and godly fear; moreover solemn humiliation *(x)* with fastings; and thanksgiving upon *(y)* special occasions, ought to be used in an holy and religious manner.
6. Neither *Prayer,* nor any other part of Religious worship, is now under the Gospel tied unto, or made more acceptable by, any place in which it is *(z)* performed, or towards which it is directed; but God is to be worshipped every where in *Spirit,* and in truth; as in (a) private families (b) daily, and (c) in secret each one by himself, so more solemnly in the publick Assemblies, which are not carelessely, nor wilfuly, to be (d) neglected, or forsaken, when God by his word, or providence calleth thereunto.

7. As it is of the Law of nature, that in general a proportion of time by Gods appointment, be set a part for the Worship of God; so by his Word in a positive-moral, and perpetual Commandment, binding all men, in all Ages, he hath particularly appointed one day in seven for a (e) *Sabbath* to be kept holy unto him, which from the beginning of the World to the Resurrection of Christ, was the last day of the week; and from the resurrection of Christ, was changed into the first day of the week (f) which is called the Lords day; and is to be continued to the end of the World, as the *Christian Sabbath;* the observation of the last day of the week being abolished.
8. The *Sabbath* is then kept holy unto the Lord, when men after a due preparing of their hearts, and ordering their common affairs aforehand, do not only observe an holy (g) rest all the day, from their own works, words, and thoughts, about their worldly employment, and recreations, but also are taken up the whole time in the publick and private exercises of his worship, and in the duties (h) of necessity and mercy.

Chapter 23: Of Lawful Oaths and Vows

Chapter 24: Of the Civil Magistrate

Chapter 25: Of Marriage

Chapter 26: Of the Church

1. The Catholick or universal Church, which (with respect to the internal work of the Spirit, and truth of grace) may be called invisible, consists of the whole (a) number of the Elect, that have been, are, or shall be gathered into one, under Christ the head thereof; and is the spouse, the body, the fulness of him that filleth all in all.
2. All persons throughout the world, professing the faith of the Gospel, and obedience unto God by Christ, according unto it; not destroying their own profession by any Errors everting the foundation, or unholyness of

conversation, *(b)* are and may be called visible Saints; *(c)* and of such ought all particular Congregations to be constituted.
3. The purest Churches under heaven are subject *(d)* to mixture, and error; and some have so degenerated as to become *(e)* no Churches of Christ, but Synagogues of Satan; nevertheless Christ always hath had, and ever shall have a *(f)* Kingdome in this world, to the end thereof, of such as believe in him, and make profession of his Name.
4. The Lord Jesus Christ is the Head of the Church, in whom by the appointment of the Father, *(g)* all power for the calling, institution, order, or Government of the Church, is invested in a supream & soveraigne manner, neither can the Pope of *Rome* in any sense be head thereof, but is *(h)* that Antichrist, that Man of sin, and Son of perdition, that exalteth himself in the Church against Christ, and all that is called God; whom the Lord shall destroy with the brightness of his coming.
5. In the execution of this power wherewith he is so intrusted, the Lord Jesus calleth out of the World unto himself, through the Ministry of his word, by his Spirit, *(i)* those that are given unto him by his Father; that they may walk before him in all the *(k)* ways of obedience, which he prescribeth to them in his Word. Those thus called he commandeth to walk together in particular societies, or *(l)* Churches, for their mutual edification; and the due performance of that publick worship, which he requireth of them in the World.
6. The Members of these Churches are *(m)* Saints by calling, visibly manifesting and evidencing (in and by their profession and walking) their obedience unto that call of Christ; and do willingly consent to walk together according to the appointment of Christ, giving up themselves, to the Lord & one to another by the will of God, *(n)* in professed subjection to the Ordinances of the Gospel.

7. To each of these Churches thus gathered, according to his mind, declared in his word, he hath given all that *(o)* power and authority, which is any way needfull, for their carrying on that order in worship, and discipline, which he hath instituted for them to observe; with commands, and rules, for the due and right exerting, and executing of that power.
8. A particular Church gathered, and compleatly Organized, according to the mind of *Christ,* consists of Officers, and Members; And the Officers appointed by Christ to be chosen and set apart by the Church (so called and gathered) for the peculiar Administration of Ordinances, and Execution of Power, or Duty, which he intrusts them with, or calls them to, to be continued to the end of the World are *(p)* Bishops or Elders and Deacons.
9. The way appointed by *Christ* for the Calling of any person, fitted, and gifted by the Holy *Spirit,* unto the Office of Bishop, or Elder, in a Church, is, that he be chosen thereunto by the common *(q)* suffrage of the Church it self; and Solemnly set apart by Fasting and Prayer, with imposition of hands of the *(r)* Eldership of the Church, if there be any before Constituted therein; And of a Deacon *(s)* that he be chosen by the like suffrage, and set apart by Prayer, and the like Imposition of hands.
10. The work of Pastors being constantly to attend the Service of *Christ,* in his Churches, in the Ministry of the Word, and Prayer, *(t)* with watching for their Souls, as they that must give an account to him; it is incumbent on the Churches to whom they Minister, not only to give them all due respect, *(u)* but also to communicate to them of all their good things according to their ability, so as they may have a comfortable supply, without being themselves *(x)* entangled in Secular Affairs; and may also be capable of exercising *(y)* Hospitality toward others; and this is required by the *(z)* Law of Nature, and by the

Express order of our Lord Jesus, who hath ordained that they that preach the Gospel, should live of the Gospel.
11. Although it be incumbent on the Bishops or Pastors of the Churches to be instant in Preaching the Word, by way of Office; yet the work of Preaching the Word, is not so peculiarly confined to them; but that others also (a) gifted, and fitted by the Holy *Spirit* for it, and approved, and called by the *Church,* may and ought to perform it.
12. As all Believers are bound to joyn themselves to particular *Churches,* when and where they have opportunity so to do; So all that are admitted unto the priviledges of a *Church,* are also (b) under the Censures and Government thereof, according to the Rule of *Christ.*
13. No Church-members upon any offence taken by them, having performed their Duty required of them towards the person they are offended at, ought to disturb any *Church* order, or absent themselves from the Assemblies of the *Church,* or Administration of any Ordinances, upon the account of such offence at any of their fellow-members; but to wait upon *Christ,* (c) in the further proceeding of the *Church.*
14. As each *Church,* and all the Members of it are bound to (d) pray continually, for the good and prosperity of all the *Churches* of *Christ,* in all places; and upon all occasions to further it (every one within the bounds of their places, and callings, in the Exercise of their Gifts and Graces) so the *Churches* (when planted by the providence of God so as they may injoy opportunity and advantage for it) ought to hold (e) communion amongst themselves for their peace, increase of love, and mutual edification.
15. In cases of difficulties or differences, either in point of Doctrine, or Administration; wherein either the Churches in general are concerned, or any one Church in their peace, union, and edification; or any member, or members, of any Church are injured, in or by any proceedings in

censures not agreeable to truth, and order: it is according to the mind of Christ, that many Churches holding communion together, do by their messengers meet to consider, (f) and give their advice, in or about that matter in difference, to be reported to all the Churches concerned; howbeit these messengers assembled are not entrusted with any Church-power properly so called; or with any jurisdiction over the Churches themselves, to exercise any censures either over any Churches, or Persons: or (g) to impose their determination on the Churches, or Officers.

Chapter 27: Of the Communion of Saints

1. All *Saints* that are united to Jesus Christ their *Head,* by his Spirit, and Faith; although they are not made thereby one person with him, have *(a)* fellowship in his Graces, sufferings, death, resurrection, and glory; and being united to one another in love, they *(b)* have communion in each others gifts, and graces; and are obliged to the performance of such duties, publick and private, in an orderly way, *(c)* as do conduce to their mutual good, both in the inward and outward man.

2. *Saints* by profession are bound to maintain an holy fellowship and communion in the worship of God, and in performing such other spiritual services, *(d)* as tend to their mutual edification; as also in relieving each other in *(e)* outward things according to their several abilities, and necessities; which communion according to the rule of the Gospel, though especially to be exercised by them, in the relations wherein they stand, whether in *(f)* families, or *(g)* Churches; yet as God offereth opportunity is to be extended to all the household of faith, even all those who in every place call upon the name of the Lord Jesus; nevertheless their communion one with another as *Saints,* doth not take away or *(h)* infringe, the title or propriety, which each man hath in his goods and possessions.

Chapter 28: Of Baptism and the Lord's Supper
1. Baptism and the Lords Supper are ordinances of positive, and soveraign institution; appointed by the Lord Jesus the only Law-giver, to be continued in his Church *(a)* to the end of the world.
2. These holy appointments are to be administered by those only, who are qualified and thereunto called according *(b)* to the commission of Christ.

Chapter 29: Of Baptism
1. Baptism is an Ordinance of the New Testament, ordained by Jesus Christ, to be unto the party Baptized, a sign of his fellowship with him, in his death, *(c)* and resurrection; of his being engrafted into him; of *(d)* remission of sins; and of his *(e)* giving up unto God through Jesus Christ to live and walk in newness of Life.
2. Those who do actually professe *(f)* repentance towards *God,* faith in, and obedience, to our Lord Jesus, are the only proper subjects of this ordinance.
3. The outward element to be used in this ordinance *(g)* is water, wherein the party is to be baptized, in the name of the Father, and of the Son, and of the Holy Spirit.
4. Immersion, or dipping of the person *(h)* in water, is necessary to the due administration of this ordinance.

Chapter 30: Of the Lord's Supper
1. The Supper of the Lord Jesus, was instituted by him, the same night wherein he was betrayed, to be observed in his Churches unto the end of the world, for the perpetual remembrance, and shewing forth the sacrifice of himself in his death *(a)* confirmation of the faith of believers in all the benefits thereof, their spiritual nourishment, and growth in him, their further ingagement in, and to, all duties which they owe unto him; *(b)* and to be a bond and pledge of their communion with him, and with each other.
2. In this ordinance Christ is not offered up to his Father, nor any real sacrifice made at all, for remission of sin of

the quick or dead; but only a memorial of that *(c)* one offering up of himself, by himself, upon the crosse, once for all; and a spiritual oblation of all *(d)* possible praise unto God for the same; so that the Popish sacrifice of the Mass (as they call it) is most abominable, injurious to Christs own only sacrifice, the alone propitiation for all the sins of the Elect.

3. The Lord Jesus hath in this Ordinance, appointed his Ministers to Pray, and bless the Elements of Bread and Wine, and thereby to set them apart from a common to an holy use, and to take and break the Bread; to take the Cup, *(e)* and (they communicating also themselves) to give both to the Communicants.

4. The denyal of the Cup to the people, worshiping the Elements, the lifting them up, or carrying them about for adoration, and reserving them for any pretended religious use, *(f)* are all contrary to the nature of this Ordinance, and to the institution of Christ.

5. The outward Elements in this Ordinance, duely set apart to the uses ordained by Christ, have such relation to him crucified, as that truely, although in terms used figuratively, they are sometimes called by the name of the things they represent, to wit the *(g)* body and Blood of Christ; albeit in substance, and nature, they still remain truly, and only *(h)* Bread, and Wine, as they were before.

6. That doctrine which maintains a change of the substance of Bread and Wine, into the substance of Christs body and blood (commonly called Transubstantiation) by consecration of a Priest, or by any other way, is repugnant not to Scripture *(i)* alone, but even to common sense and reason; overthroweth the *(k)* nature of the ordinance, and hath been and is the cause of manifold superstitions, yea, of gross Idolatries.

7. Worthy receivers, outwardly partaking of the visible Elements in this Ordinance, do then also inwardly by faith, really and indeed, yet not carnally, and corporally, but

spiritually receive, and feed upon Christ crucified *(l)* & all the benefits of his death: the Body and Blood of *Christ*, being then not corporally, or carnally, but spiritually present to the faith of Believers, in that Ordinance, as the Elements themselves are to their outward senses.
8. All ignorant and ungodly persons, as they are unfit to enjoy communion *(m)* with *Christ;* so are they unworthy of the Lords Table; and cannot without great sin against him, while they remain such, partake of these holy mysteries, *(n)* or be admitted thereunto: yea whosoever shall receive unworthily are guilty of the Body and Blood of the Lord, eating and drinking judgement to themselves.

Chapter 31: Of the State of Man After Death and of the Resurrection of the Dead

1. The Bodies of Men after Death return to dust, *(a)* and see corruption; but their Souls (which neither die nor sleep) having an immortal subsistence, immediately *(b)* return to God who gave them: the Souls of the Righteous being then made perfect in holyness, are received into paradise where they are with *Christ*, and behold the face of *God,* in light *(c)* and glory; waiting for the full Redemption of their Bodies; and the souls of the wicked, are cast into hell; where they remain in torment and utter darkness, reserved to *(d)* the judgement of the great day; besides these two places for Souls separated from their bodies, the Scripture acknowledgeth none.
2. At the last day such of the Saints as are found alive shall not sleep but be *(e)* changed; and all the dead shall be raised up with the self same bodies, and *(f)* none other; although with different *(g)* qualities, which shall be united again to their Souls for ever.
3. The bodies of the unjust shall by the power of *Christ*, be raised to dishonour; the bodies of the just by his spirit unto honour, *(h)* and be made conformable to his own glorious Body.

Chapter 32: Of the Last Judgement

1. God hath appointed a Day wherein he will judge the world in Righteousness, by *(a)* Jesus Christ; to whom all power and judgement is given of the Father; in which Day not only the *(b)* Apostate Angels shall be judged; but likewise all persons that have lived upon the Earth, shall appear before the Tribunal of *Christ; (c)* to give an account of their Thoughts, Words, and Deeds, and to receive according to what they have done in the body, whether good or evil.
2. The end of Gods appointing this Day, is for the manifestation of the glory of his Mercy, in the Eternal Salvation of the Elect; *(d)* and of his Justice in the Eternal damnation of the Reprobate, who are wicked and disobedient; for then shall the Righteous go into Everlasting Life, and receive that fulness of Joy, and Glory, with everlasting reward, in the presence *(e)* of the Lord: but the wicked who know not God, and obey not the Gospel of Jesus Christ, shall be cast into Eternal torments, and *(f)* punished with everlasting destruction, from the presence of the Lord, and from the glory of his power.
3. As Christ would have us to be certainly perswaded that there shall be a Day of judgement, both *(g)* to deter all men from sin, and for the greater *(h)* consolation of the godly, in their adversity; so will he have that day unknown to Men, that they may shake off all carnal security, and be always watchful, because they know not at what hour, the *(i)* Lord will come; and may ever be prepared to say, *(k) Come Lord Jesus, Come quickly, Amen.*

An Appendix

Whosoever reads, and impartially considers what we have in our forgoing confession declared, may readily perceive, That we do not only concenter with all other true Christians on the Word of God (revealed in the Scriptures of truth) as the foundation and rule of our faith and worship. But that we have also industriously endeavoured to manifest, That in the fundamental Articles of Christianity we mind the same things, and have therefore expressed our belief in the same words, that have on the like occasion been spoken by other societies of Christians before us.

This we have done, That those who are desirous to know the principles of Religion which we hold and practise, may take an estimate from our selves (who jointly concur in this work) and may not be misguided, either by undue reports; or by the ignorance or errors of particular persons, who going under the same name with our selves, may give an occasion of scandalizing the truth we profess.

And although we do differ from our brethren who are Paedobaptists; in the subject and administration of Baptisme, and such other circumstances as have a necessary dependence on our observance of that Ordinance, and do frequent our own assemblies for our mutual edification, and discharge of those duties, and services which we owe unto God, and in his fear to each other: yet we would not be from hence misconstrued, as if the discharge of our own consciences herein, did any wayes disoblige or alienate our affections, or conversation from any others that fear the Lord; but that we may and do as we have opportunity participate of the labors of those, whom God hath indued with abilities above our selves, and qualified, and called to the Ministry of the *Word,* earnestly desiring to approve our selves to be such, as follow after peace with holyness, and therefore we always keep that blessed *Irenicum,* or healing *Word* of the Apostle before our eyes; if in any thing ye be otherwise minded, God shall reveal even this unto you; nevertheless whereto we have already attained; let us walk by the same rule, let us mind the same thing, *Phil* 3. *v.* 15,16.

Let it not therefore be judged of us (because much hath been written on this subject, and yet we continue this our practise different from others) that it is out of obstinacy, but rather as the truth is, that we do herein according to the best of our understandings worship God, out of a pure mind yielding obedience to his precept, in that method which we take to be most agreeable to the Scriptures of truth, and primitive practise.

It would not become us to give any such intimation, as should carry a semblance that what we do in the service of God is with a doubting conscience, or with any such temper of mind that we do thus for the present, with a reservation that we will do otherwise hereafter upon more mature deliberation; nor have we any cause so to do, being fully perswaded, that what we do is agreeable to the will of God. Yet we do heartily propose this, that if any of the Servants of our Lord Jesus shall, in the Spirit of meekness, attempt to convince us of any mistake either in judgement or practise, we shall diligently ponder his arguments; and accompt him our chiefest friend that shall be an instrument to convert us from any error that is in our ways, for we cannot wittingly do any thing against the truth, but all things for the truth.

And therefore we have indeavoured seriously to consider, what hath been already offered for our satisfaction in this point; and are loth to say any more lest we should be esteemed desirous of renewed contests thereabout: yet forasmuch as it may justly be expected that we shew some reason, why we cannot acquiesce in what hath been urged against us; we shall with as much brevity as may consist with plainness, endeavour to satisfie the expectation of those that shall peruse what we now publish in this matter also.

1. As to those Christians who consent with us, *That Repentance from dead works, and Faith towards God, and our Lord Jesus Christ, is required in persons to be Baptized;* and do therefore supply the defect of the (infant being uncapable of making confession of either) by others who do undertake these things for it. Although we do find by Church history that this hath been a very antient practise; yet considering, that the same Scripture which

does caution us against censuring our brother, with whom we shall all stand before the judgment seat of Christ, does also instruct us, *That every one of us shall give an accompt of himself to God, and whatsoever is not of Faith is Sin.* Rom. 14:4,10,12,23. Therefore we cannot for our own parts be perswaded in our own minds, to build such a practise as this, upon an unwritten tradition: But do rather choose in all points of Faith and Worship, to have recourse to the holy Scriptures, for the information of our judgment, and regulation of our practise; being well assured that a conscientious attending thereto, is the best way to prevent, and rectifie our defects and errors. 2 *Tim.* 3.16,17. And if any such case happen to be debated between Christians, which is not plainly determinable by the Scriptures, we think it safest to leave such things undecided until the second coming of our Lord Jesus; as they did in the Church of old, until there should arise a Priest with *Urim* and *Thummim,* that might certainly inform them of the mind of God thereabout, *Ezra* 2.62,63.

2. As for those our Christian brethren who do ground their arguments for Infants baptism, upon a presumed faederal Holiness, or Church-Membership, we conceive they are deficient in this, that albeit this Covenant-Holiness and Membership should be as is supposed, in reference unto the Infants of Believers; yet no command for Infant baptism does immediately and directly result from such a quality, or relation.

All instituted Worship receives its sanction from the precept, and is to be thereby governed in all the necessary circumstances thereof.

So it was in the Covenant that God made with *Abraham* and his Seed. The sign whereof was appropriated only to the Male, notwithstanding that the female seed as well as the Male were comprehended in the Covenant and part of the Church of God; neither was this sign to be affixed to any Male Infant till he was eight dayes old, albeit he was within the Covenant from the first moment of his life; nor could the danger of death, or any other supposed necessity, warrant the circumcising of him before the set time, nor was there any cause for it; the commination of being cut off from his people, being only upon the neglect, or contempt of the precept.

Righteous *Lot* was nearly related to *Abraham* in the flesh, and contemporary with him, when this Covenant was made; yet inasmuch as he did not descend from his loynes, nor was of his household family (although he was of the same household of faith with *Abraham*) yet neither *Lot* himself nor any of his posterity (because of their descent from him) were signed with the signature of this Covenant that was made with *Abraham* and his seed.

This may suffice to shew, that where there was both an expresse Covenant, and a sign thereof (such a Covenant as did separate the persons with whom it was made, and all their off-spring from all the rest of the world, as a people holy unto the Lord, and did constitute them the visible Church of God, (though not comprehensive of all the faithful in the world) yet the sign of this Covenant was not affixed to all the persons that were within this Covenant, nor to any of them till the prefixt season; nor to other faithful servants of God, that were not of descent from *Abraham*. And consequently that it depends purely upon the will of the Law-giver, to determine what shall be the sign of his Covenant, unto whom, at what season, and upon what terms, it shall be affixed.

If our brethren do suppose baptism to be the seal of the Covenant which God makes with every believer (of which the Scriptures are altogether silent) it is not our concern to contend with them herein; yet we conceive the seal of that Covenant is the indwelling of the Spirit of Christ in the particular and individual persons in whom he resides, and nothing else, neither do they or we suppose that baptism is in any such manner substituted in the place of circumcision, as to have the same (and no other) latitude, extent, or terms, then circumcision had; for that was suited only for the Male children, baptism is an ordinance suited for every believer, whether male, or femal. That extended to all the males that were born in *Abrahams* house, or bought with his money, equally with the males that proceeded from his own loynes; but baptisme is not so far extended in any true Christian Church that we know of, as to be administred to all the poor infidel servants, that the members thereof purchase for their service, and introduce into their families; nor to the children born of them in their house.

But we conceive the same parity of reasoning may hold for the ordinance of baptism as for that of circumcision; *Exodus* 12.49. *viz.* one law for the stranger, as for the home born: If any desire to be admitted to all the ordinances, and priviledges of Gods house, the door is open; upon the same terms that any one person was ever admitted to all, or any of those priviledges, that belong to the Christian Church; may all persons of right challenge the like admission.

As for that text of Scripture, Rom. 4.11. *He received circumcision a seal of the righteousness of the faith which he had yet being uncircumcised;* we conceive if the Apostles scope in that place be duly attended to, it will appear that no argument can be taken from thence to inforce Infant baptism; and forasmuch as we find a full and fair account of those words given by the learned Dr. *Lighfoot* (a man not to be suspected of partiality in this controversie) in his *Hor. Hebrai,* on the 1 *Cor.* 7.19. *p.* 42,43. we shall transcribe his words at large, without any comment of our own upon them.

Circumcision is nothing, if we respect the time, for now it was without use, that end of it being especially fulfilled; for which it had been instituted: this end the Apostle declares in these words, *Rom.* 4.11 σπηραγιδα. But I fear that by most translations they are not sufficiently suited to the end of circumcision, and the scope of the Apostle whilst something of their own is by them inserted.

And after the Doctor hath represented diverse versions of the words agreeing for the most part in sense with that which we have in our Bibles he thus proceeds.

Other versions are to the same purpose; as if circumcision was given to *Abraham* for a Seal of that Righteousness which he had being yet uncircumcised, which we will not deny to be in some sense true, but we believe that circumcision had chiefly a far different respect.

Give me leave thus to render the words; *And he received the sign of circumcision, a seal of the Righteousness of Faith, which was to be in the uncircumcision, Which was to be* (I say) not *which had been,* not that which *Abraham* had whilst he was yet uncircumcised; but that which his uncircumcised seed should have, that is the Gentiles, who in time to come should imitate the faith of *Abraham.*

Now consider well on what occasion circumcision was instituted unto *Abraham,* setting before thine eyes the history thereof, *Gen. 17.*

This promise is first made unto him, *Thou shalt be the Father of many Nations* (in what sense the Apostle explaineth in that chapter) and then there is subjoined a double seal for the confirmation of the thing, to wit, the change of the name *Abram* into *Abraham,* and the institution of circumcision. v 4. *Behold as for me, my Covenant is with thee, and thou shalt be the Father of many Nations.* Wherefore was his name called *Abraham?* for the sealing of this promise. *Thou shalt be the Father of many Nations.* And wherefore was circumcision instituted to him? For the sealing of the same promise. Thou shalt be the Father of many Nations. So that this is the sense of the Apostle; most agreeable to the institution of circumcision; he received the sign of circumcision, a seal of the Righteousness of Faith which in time to come the uncircumcision (or the Gentiles) should have and obtain.

Abraham had a twofold seed, *natural,* of the Jews; and *faithful,* of the believing Gentiles: his natural seed was signed with the sign of circumcision, first indeed for the distinguishing of them from all other Nations whilst they as yet were not the seed of *Abraham,* but especially for the memorial of the justification of the Gentiles by faith, when at length they should become his seed. Therefore circumcision was of right to cease, when the Gentiles were brought in to the faith, forasmuch as then it had obtained its last and chief end, & thenceforth circumcision is nothing.

Thus far he, which we earnestly desire may be seriously weighed, for we plead not his authority, but the evidence of truth in his words.

   3. Of whatsoever nature the holiness of the children mentioned, 1 *Cor.* 7. 12. be, yet they who do conclude that all such children (whether Infants or of riper years) have from hence an immediate right to baptism, do as we conceive put more into the conclusion, then will be found in the premisses.

For although we do not determine positively concerning the Apostles scope in the holiness here mentioned, so as to say it is this, or that, and no other thing; Yet it is evident that the Apostle does by it determine not only the lawfulness but the expedience also of a believers cohabitation with an unbeliever, in the state of marriage.

And we do think that although the Apostles asserting of the unbelieving yokefellow to be sanctified by the believer, should carry in it somewhat more then is in the bare marriage of two infidels, because although the marriage covenant have a divine sanction so as to make the wedlock of two unbelievers a lawful action, and their conjunction and cohabitation in that respect undefiled, yet there might be no ground to suppose from thence, that both or either of their persons are thereby sanctified; and the Apostle urges the cohabitation of a believer with an infidel in the state of wedlock from this ground that the unbelieving husband is *sanctified* by the believing wife; nevertheless here you have the influence of a believers faith *ascending from an inferior to a superior relation;* from the wife to the husband who is her head, *before it can descend to their off-spring.* And therefore we say, whatever be the nature or extent of the holiness here intended, we conceive it cannot convey to the children an immediate right to baptism; because it would then be of another nature, and of a larger extent, then the root, and original from whence it is derived, for it is clear by the Apostles argument that holiness cannot be derived to the child from the sanctity of one parent only, if either father or mother be (in the sense intended by the Apostle) unholy or unclean, so will the child be also, therefore for the production of an holy seed it is necessary that both the Parents be sanctified; and this the Apostle positively asserts in the first place to be done by the believing parent, although the other be an unbeliever; and then consequentially from thence argues, the holiness of their children. Hence it follows, that as the children have no other holiness then what they derive from both their Parents; so neither can they have any right by this holiness to any spiritual priviledge but such as both their Parents did also partake of: and therefore if the unbelieving Parent (though sanctified by the believing Parent) have not thereby a right to baptism, neither can we conceive, that there is any such priviledge, derived to the children by their birth-holiness.

Besides if it had been the usual practice in the Apostles dayes for the father or mother that did believe, to bring all their children with them to be baptised; then the holiness of the believing *Corinthians* children, would not at all have been in question when this Epistle was written; but might have been argued from their passing under that ordinance, which represented their new birth, although they had derived no holiness from their Parents, by their first birth; and would have layen as an exception against the Apostles inference, *else were your Children unclean,* &c. But of the sanctification of all the children of every believer by this ordinance, or any other way, then what is beforementioned, the Scripture is altogether silent.

This may also be added; that if this birth holiness do qualifie all the children of every believer, for the ordinance of baptism; why not for all other ordinances? for the Lords Supper as was practiced for a long time together? for if recourse be had to what the Scriptures speak generally of this subject; it will be found, that the same qualities which do intitle any person to baptism, do so also for the participation of all the Ordinances, and priviledges of the house of God, that are common to all believers.

Whosoever can and does interrogate his good Conscience towards God when he is baptised (as every one must do that makes it to himself a sign of Salvation) is capable of doing the same thing, in every other act of worship that he performs.

    4. The arguments and inferences that are usually brought for, or against Infant baptism from those few instances which the Scriptures afford us of whole families being baptised; are only conjectural; and therefore cannot of themselves, be conclusive on either hand: yet in regard most that treat on this subject for Infant baptism, do (as they conceive) improve these instances to the advantage of their argument: we think it meet (in like manner as in the cases before mentioned so in this) to shew the invalidity of such inferences.

Cornelius worshipped God with all his house, the *Jaylor,* and *Crispus* the chief ruler of the Synagogue, *believed God with each of their houses. The houshold of* Stephanus *addicted themselves to the Ministry of the Saints:* so that thus far *Worshipping,* and *Believing* runs parallel with *Baptism.* And if *Lydia,* had been a married person, when she believed, it is probable her husband would also have been named by the Apostle, as in like cases, inasmuch as he would have been not only a part, but the head of that baptised household.

Who can assign any probable reason, why the Apostle should make mention of four or five households being baptised and no more? or why he does so often vary in the method of his salutations, *Rom.* 1. 6. sometimes mentioning only particular persons of great note, other times such, and the Church in their house? the Saints that were with them; and them belonging to

Narcissus, who were in the Lord; thus saluting either whole families, or part of families, or only particular persons in families, considered as they were in the Lord, for if it had been an usual practise to baptize all children, with their parents; there were then many thousands of the Jews which believed, and a great number of the Gentiles, in most of the principle Cities in the World, and among so many thousands, it is more then probable there would have been some thousands of households baptised; why then should the Apostle in this respect signalize one family of the Jews and three or four of the Gentiles, as particular instances in a case that was common? whoever supposes that we do willfully debar our children, from the benefit of any promise, or priviledge, that of right belongs to the children of believing parents; they do entertain over severe thoughts of us: to be without natural affections is one of the characters of the worst of persons; in the worst of times. We do freely confess our selves guilty before the Lord, in that we have not with more circumspection and diligence train'd up those that relate to us in the fear of the Lord; and do humbly and earnestly pray, that our omissions herein may be remitted, and that they may not redound to the prejudice of our selves, or any of ours: but with respect to that duty that is incumbent on us, we acknowledge our selves obliged by the precepts of God, to bring up our children in the nurture and admonition of the Lord, to teach them his fear, both by instruction and example; and should we set light by this precept, it would demonstrate that we are more vile then the unnatural Heathen, that like not to retain God in their knowledge, our baptism might then be justly accompted, as no baptism to us.

There are many special promises that do incourage us as well as precepts, that do oblige us to the close pursuit of our duty herein: that God whom we serve, being jealous of his Worship, threatens the visiting of the Fathers transgression upon the children to the third and fourth generation of them that hate him: yet does more abundantly extend his mercy, even to thousands (respecting the offspring and succeding generations) of them that love him, and keep his commands.

When our Lord rebuked his disciples for prohibiting the access of little children that were brought to him, that he might pray over them, lay his hands upon them, and blesse them, does declare, *that of such is the Kingdom of God.* And the Apostle *Peter* in answer to their enquiry, that desired to know what they must do to be saved, does not only instruct them in the necessary duty of repentance and baptism; but does also thereto encourage them, by that promise which had reference both to them, and their children; if our Lord Jesus in the forementioned place, do not respect the qualities of children (as elsewhere) as to their meekness, humility, and sincerity, and the like; but intend also that those very persons and such like, appertain to the Kingdom of God, and if the Apostle *Peter* in mentioning the aforesaid promise, do respect not only the present and succeeding generations of those Jews, that heard him, (in which sense the same phrase doth occurre in Scripture) but also the immediate off-spring of his auditors; whether the promise relate to the gift of the Holy Spirit, or of eternal life, or any grace, or priviledge tending to the obtaining thereof; it is neither our concerne nor our interest to confine the mercies, and promises of God, to a more narrow, or lesse compasse then he is pleased gratiously to offer and intend them; nor to have a light esteem of them; but are obliged in duty to God, and affection to our children; to plead earnestly with God and use our utmost endeavours that both our selves, and our off-spring may be partakers of his Mercies and gracious Promises: yet we cannot from either of these texts collect a sufficient warrant for us to baptize our children before they are instructed in the principles of the Christian Religion.

For as to the instance in little children, it seems by the disciples forbidding them, that they were brought upon some other account, not so frequent as Baptism must be supposed to have been, if from the beginning believers children had been admitted thereto: and no account is given whether their parents were baptised believers or not; and as to the instance of the Apostle; if the following words and practice, may be taken as an interpretation of the scope of that promise we cannot conceive it does refer to infant baptism, because the text does presently subjoyn; *Then they that gladly received the word were baptised.*

That there were some believing children of believing parents in the Apostles dayes is evident from the Scriptures, even such as were then in ther fathers family, and under their parents tuition, and education; to whom the Apostle in several of his Epistles to the Churches, giveth commands to obey their parents in the Lord; and does allure their tender years to hearken to this precept, by reminding them that it is the first command with promise.

And it is recorded by him for the praise of *Timothy,* and encouragement of parents betimes to instruct, and children early to attend to godly instruction, that from a child, he had known the holy Scriptures.

The Apostle *John* rejoyced greatly when he found of the children of the Elect Lady walking in the truth; and the children of her Elect Sister joyn with the Apostle in his salutation.

But that this was not generally so, that all the children of believers were accounted for believers (as they would have been if they had been all baptised) may be collected from the character which the Apostle gives of persons fit to be chosen to Eldership in the Church which was not common to all believers; among others this is expressely one, *viz. If there be any having believing, or faithful children,* not accused of Riot or unruly; and we may from the Apostles writings on the same subject collect the reason of this qualification, *viz.* That in case the person designed for this office to teach and rule in the house of God, had children capable of it; there might be first a proof of his ability, industry, and successe in this work in his own family; and private capacity, before he was ordained to the exercise of this authority in the Church, in a publick capacity, as a Bishop in the house of God.

These things we have mentioned as having a direct reference unto the controversie between our brethren and us; other things that are more abstruse and prolix, which are frequently introduced into this controversie, but do not necessarily concern it, we have purposely avoided; that the distance between us and our brethren may not be by us made more wide; for it is our duty, and concern so far as is possible for us (retaining a good conscience towards God) to seek a more entire agreement and reconciliation with them.

We are not insenible that as to the order of Gods house, and entire communion therein there are some things wherein we (as well as others) are not at a full accord among our selves, as for instance; the known principle, and state of the consciences of diverse of us, that have agreed in this Confession is such; that we cannot hold Church-communion, with any other then Baptized-believers, and Churches constituted of such; yet some others of us have a greater liberty and freedom in our spirits that way; and therefore we have purposely omitted the mention of things of that nature, that we might concurre, in giving this evidence of our agreement, both among our selves, and with other good Christians, in those important articles of the Christian Religion, mainly insisted on by us: and this notwithstanding we all esteem it our chief concern, both among our selves, and all others that in every place call upon the name of the Lord Jesus Christ our Lord, both theirs and ours, and love him in sincerity, to endeavour to keep the unity of the Spirit, in the bond of peace; and in order thereunto, to exercise all lowliness and meekness, with long-suffering, forbearing one another in love.

And we are perswaded if the same method were introduced into frequent practice between us and our Christian friends who agree with us in all the fundamental articles of the

Christian faith (though they do not so in the subject and administration of baptism) it would soon beget a better understanding, and brotherly affection between us.

In the beginning of the Christian Church, when the doctrine of the baptism of *Christ* was not universally understood, yet those that knew only the baptism of *John,* were the Disciples of the Lord Jesus; and *Apollos* an eminent Minister of the Gospel of Jesus.

In the beginning of the reformation of the Christian Church, and recovery from that *Egyptian* darkness wherein our forefathers for many generations were held in bondage; upon recourse had to the Scriptures of truth, different apprehensions were conceived, which are to this time continued, concerning the practise of this Ordinance.

Let not our zeal herein be misinterpreted: that God whom we serve is jealous of his worship. By his gracious providence the Law thereof, is continued amongst us; and we are forewarned by what hapned in the Church of the Jews, that it is necessary for every generation, and that frequently in every generation to consult the divine oracle, compare our worship with the rule, and take heed to what doctrines we receive and practise.

If the ten commands exhibited in the popish Idolatrous service books had been received as the entire law of God, because they agree in number with his ten commands, and also in the substance of nine of them; the second Commandment forbidding Idolatry had been utterly lost.

If *Ezra* and *Nehemiah* had not made a diligent search into the particular parts of Gods law, and his worship; the Feast of Tabernacles (which for many centuries of years, had not been duly observed, according to the institution, though it was retained in the general notion) would not have been kept in due order.

So may it be now as to many things relating to the service of God, which do retain the names proper to them in their first institution, but yet through inadvertency (where there is no sinister design) may vary in their circumstances, from their first institution. And if by means of any antient defection, or of that general corruption of the service of God, and interruption of his true worship, and persecution of his servants by the Antichristian Bishop of *Rome,* for many generations; those who do consult the Word of God, cannot yet arrive at a full and mutual satisfaction among themselves, what was the practise of the primitive Christian Church, in some points relating to the *Worship* of God: yet inasmuch as these things are not of the essence of Christianity, but that we agree in the fundamental doctrines thereof, we do apprehend, there is sufficient ground to lay aside all bitterness and prejudice, and in the spirit of love and meekness to imbrace and own each other therein; leaving each other at liberty to perform such other services, (wherein we cannot concur) apart unto God, according to the best of our understanding.

Finis

Subscribers to the Confession of Faith

We the Ministers, and Messengers of, and concerned for upwards of, one hundred Baptised Churches, in England and Wales (denying Arminianism), being met together in London, from the third of the seventh month to the eleventh of the same, 1689, to consider of some things that might be for the glory of God, and the good of these congregations, have thought meet (for the satisfaction of all other Christians that differ from us in the point of Baptism) to recommend to their perusal the confession of our faith, which confession we own, as containing the doctrine of our faith and practice, and do desire that the members of our churches respectively do furnish themselves therewith.

[Then follows a list of the subscribers with links to their personal information.]

ENDNOTES

Please note that URLs for Internet sources were accurate as of the time of publication. Some links, however, may have changed or expired since that time.

[1] Haddon W. Robinson, *Making a Difference in Preaching* (Grand Rapids MI: Baker Books, 1999), pp. 36,37.

[2] Ibid.

[3] Herschel H. Hobbs, *The Baptist Faith and Message* (Nashville TN: Convention Press, 1971), p. 121.

[4] Hobbs, *The Baptist Faith,* p. 127.

[5] "The Baptist Faith and Message," adopted by the Southern Baptist Convention, May 9, 1963, p. 5.

[6] Some also maintain that Matthew 11:12 ("From the days of John the Baptist until now, the kingdom of heaven has been forcefully advancing, and forceful men lay hold of it.") shows the historical extent of the true Baptist church and proves their point.

[7] J. R. Graves, *Old Landmarkism, What Is It?* (Baptist Book House, 1880).

[8] *The Book of Concord: The Confessions of the Evangelical Lutheran Church,* translated and edited by Theodore G. Tappert (Philadelphia: Fortress Press, 1959), p. 498.

[9] "World News," *Forward in Christ,* Vol. 91, No. 6 (June 2004), p. 28.

[10] http://www.pb.org/pbfaq.html.

[11] http://www.wordofhisgrace.org/ArminianQA.htm.

[12] James Savastio, "What Is a Reformed Baptist Church?" http://www.prbc.org/ReformedBaptist.htm.

[13] http://www.wordofhisgrace.org/ArminianQA.htm.

[14] See the *Confessional Statement of the Baptist Church* (1689), Chapter 3, "God's Decree": "Those of mankind that are predestinated to life, God, before the foundation of the world was laid, according to his eternal and immutable purpose, and the secret counsel and good pleasure of his will, hath chosen in Christ unto everlasting glory, out of his mere free grace and love, without any other thing in the creature as a condition or cause moving him thereunto." www.vor.org/truth/1689/1689bc00.html.

[15] "The 1689 London Confession of Faith," paragraph 34, www.vor.org/truth/1689/1689bc00.html.

[16] http://www.adherents.com/largecom/com_sbc.html.

[17] http://www.sbc.net/aboutus/default.asp.

[18] http://www.abc-usa.org/whoweare/default.aspx.

[19] http://www.abc-usa.org/whoweare/default.aspx.

[20] From the "Policy Statement on Denominational Inclusivesness" adopted by the General Board of the American Baptist Churches, June 1993.

[21] Statement of the Executive Committee of the General Board, September 1995, http://www.abc-usa.org.

[22] "Two Baptist Churches That Welcome Gays Escape Expulsion," *Seattle Times* (May 21, 2000).

[23] This was adopted by the General Board of the American Baptist Churches by Mail Vote, October 1992.

[24] http://www.abcosh.org/resourses/pdf/ABCUSA_Homosexuality.pdf (11/2008).

[25] Doctrinal Statement, XIX, http://www.garbc.org/news/?page id=31.

[26] http://www.generalbaptist.com/Council%20of%20Assoc/Statements%20of%20Faith.htm.

[27] Ibid.

[28] Ministry Objectives of the NBCA, http://www.nbcamerica.net/ministry.htm.

[29] http://www.puritanhope.com/arbca/.

[30] http://www.vor.org/truth/1689/1689bc00.html.

[31] "Statement of Faith," Trinity Reformed Baptist Church, Baltimore, Maryland.

[32] Savastio, "What Is a Reformed Baptist Church?" http://www.prbc.org/ReformedBaptist.htm.

[33] http://www.pb.org/pbfaq.html.

[34] Ibid.

[35] http://www.seventhdaybaptist.org.

[36] For more information on the Separate Baptist Churches, see http://www.separatebaptist.org/index.php?page=genglance.

[37] http://en.wikipedia.org/wiki/United_Baptist.

[38] http://en.wikipedia.org/wiki/Two-Seed-in-the-Spirit_Predestinarian_Baptists.

[39] http://spbaptist.tripod.com/synopsis.html.

[40] Alan Siggelkow, "Pastoral Leadership From the Perspective of Church History," *Wisconsin Lutheran Quarterly,* Vol. 101, No. 3 (Summer 2004), p. 181.

[41] Hobbs, *The Baptist Faith,* p. 105.

[42] Ibid.

[43] "The Baptist Faith and Message," adopted 1963, p. 7.

[44] http://www.sbc.net/bfm/default.asp.

[45] Michael Foust, "Historical Confessions Guard Against Heresy, Leaders Say," *Baptist Press* (April 22, 2004).

[46] E-mail from Rev. Paul McCain, Subject: "A Remarkable Affirmation of Creeds by Russell D. Moore."

[47] Morris H. Chapman, President and Chief Executive Officer, SBC Executive Committee, "SBC Committee on Nominations Begins Its Work—Here's What You Can Do," *Journal of the Southern Baptist Convention,* November 2004.

[48] Patsy Leppian and J. Kincaid Smith, *What's Going On Among the Lutherans?* (Milwaukee WI: Northwestern Publishing House, 1992), p. 225.

[49] "Ordained Southern Baptist Women," http://www.wayoflife.org.

[50] "Female Baptist Pastor Leads to Controversy," Louise Chu, Associated Press, September 24, 2004.

[51] Savastio, "What Is a Reformed Baptist Church?" http://www.prbc.org/ReformedBaptist.htm.

[52] Ibid.

[53] Martin Luther, *What Luther Says: An Anthology*, compiled by Ewald M. Plass, Vol. 3 (St. Louis MO: Concordia Publishing House, 1959), p. 1163.

[54] Leppian and Smith, *What's Going On Among the Lutherans?* p. 227. The authors here quote from John Calvin, *Institutes of the Christian Religion I*, VIII:2.

[55] "The Baptist Faith and Message," adopted 1963, p. 8.

[56] http://www.prbc.org/ReformedBaptist.htm.

[57] "The Baptist Faith and Message," adopted 1963, pp. 16,17.

[58] http://www.prbc.org/ReformedBaptist.htm.

[59] John Brug, "The Lutheran Doctrine of Sanctification and Its Rivals," *Wisconsin Lutheran Quarterly*, Vol. 101, No. 3 (Summer 2004), p. 191.

[60] Brug, "The Lutheran Doctrine of Sanctification," pp. 197,198.

[61] "The Baptist Faith and Message," adopted 1963, pp. 10,11.

[62] Billy Graham, *How to Be Born Again* (New York: Warner Books, 1977), pp. 162,169.

[63] "The Baptist Faith and Message," adopted 1963, p. 12.

[64] Leppian and Smith, *What's Going On Among the Lutherans?* pp. 230,231. The authors are quoting Lewis Spitz, *Our Church and Others* (St. Louis: Concordia Publishing House, 1960), p. 69.

[65] "The Baptist Faith and Message," adopted 1963, p. 13.

[66] From the 1644 London Confession, Article XL, http://www.spurgeon.org/~phil/creeds/bc1644.htm.

[67] Adopted in substance by vote at the SBC Convention in Cincinnati, Ohio, May 15, 1970.

[68] Hobbs, *The Baptist Faith*, p. 87.

[69] "Baptism: A Washing for All Time," from the series For Living Saints (Milwaukee WI: Northwestern Publishing House, 2003).

[70] *A Baptist Catechism*, http://www.desiringgod.org/AboutUs/OurDistinctives/ABaptistCatechism/.

[71] Andrew Das, *Baptized Into God's Family* (Milwaukee WI: Northwestern Publishing House, 1991), p. 9, quoting Uuras Saarnivaara, *Scriptural Baptism* (New York: Vantage Press, 1953).

[72] "The Baptist Faith and Message," adopted 1963, p. 10.

[73] David Vallesky, "Evangelical Lutheranism and Today's Evangelicals and Fundamentalists," *Wisconsin Lutheran Quarterly*, Vol. 80, No. 3 (Summer 1983), p. 207.

[74] Free Will Baptist Web site:
http://www.holywordcafe.com/fwb/treatisefaith.html#I.

[75] "The 1689 Confession of Faith," Chapter 15,
http://www.prbc.org/ReformedBaptist.htm (Note: The 1689 confession can be found in various places on the Internet. The source here is an alternate to the one used earlier.)

[76] Ibid.

[77] http://www.wayoflife.org/fbns/bewareof-lutheran-infbap.html.

[78] The Reformed (Baptist) teaching is called *Representation*. They believe that Jesus' body and blood are represented by the bread and the wine. The Roman Catholic belief on the Lord's Supper is called *Transubstantiation*. They believe that the bread and wine actually cease being bread and wine and literally turn into the body and blood of Christ.

[79] The Large Catechism, *The Book of Concord: The Confessions of the Evangelical Lutheran Church*, translated and edited by Theodore G. Tappert, (Philadelphia: Fortress Press, 1959), p. 448.

[80] Francis Pieper, *Christian Dogmatics*, Vol. 3, (St. Louis: Concordia Publishing House, 1953), p. 295, quoting from the *Consensus Tigurinus*, XXII.

[81] Leppian and Smith, *What's Going On Among the Lutherans?* p. 228, quoting David Jay Webber.

[82] "The Baptist Faith and Message," adopted 1963, p. 13.

[83] Hobbs, *The Baptist Faith*, p. 88.

[84] Hobbs, *The Baptist Faith*, pp. 89,90.

[85] Hobbs, *The Baptist Faith*, p. 90.

[86] Article XVIII was added in 1998 and now appears in the 2000 "Baptist Faith and Message." http://www.sbc.net/bfm/bfm2000.asp#xviii.

[87] "The 1689 Confession of Faith," Chapter 25: "Of Marriage," http://www.prbc.org/Confession.htm#Chapter%2025.

[88] http://www.sbc.net.

[89] "Baptist Faith and Message," Article XV, "The Christian and the Social Order," http://www.sbc.net/bfm/default.asp.

[90] SBC Resolutions, "Resolution on Divorce," May 1904, www.sbc.net.

[91] Armin Schuetze and Irwin Habeck, *The Shepherd Under Christ* (Milwaukee WI: Northwestern Publishing House, 1974), p. 287.

[92] "The 1689 Confession of Faith," Chapter 9: "Of Free Will," http://www.prbc.org/Confession.htm.

[93] "The 1689 Confession of Faith," Chapter 10: "Of Effectual Calling," http://www.prbc.org/Confession.htm.

[94] "The 1689 Confession of Faith," Chapter 16: "Of Good Works," http://www.prbc.org/Confession.htm.

[95] Savastio, "What Is a Reformed Baptist Church?" http://www.prbc.org/ReformedBaptist.htm.

ENDNOTES

[96] David P. Kuske, *Luther's Catechism*, WELS Board for Parish Services (Milwaukee WI: Northwestern Publishing House, 1982), p. 67.
[97] Savastio, "What Is a Reformed Baptist Church?" http://www.prbc.org/ReformedBaptist.htm.
[98] SBC "Resolution on Keeping the Lord's Day," Indianapolis, Indiana, June 1992.
[99] Brug, "The Lutheran Doctrine of Sanctification," p. 189.
[100] Vallesky, "Evangelical Lutheranism," p. 198.
[101] Graham, *How to Be Born Again*, p. 169.
[102] "The 1689 Confession of Faith," http://www.prbc.org/ReformedBaptist.htm.
[103] Kuske, *Luther's Catechism*, The Third Article of the Apostles' Creed: *"What does this mean?"* p. 5.
[104] Position Statements: Autonomy, http://www.sbc.net.
[105] Hobbs, *The Baptist Faith*, p. 111.
[106] http://www.lcms.org.
[107] Savastio, "What Is a Reformed Baptist Church?" http://www.prbc.org/ReformedBaptist.htm.
[108] From the revised 2000 "Baptist Faith and Message," Article VI, adopted June 14, 2000, http://www.sbc.net/bfm/default.asp.
[109] http://www.sbc.net/redirect.asp?url=http://www.sbcannualmeeting.org/sbc00/news.asp?ID=1927611432.
[110] Ibid.
[111] From "The American Baptist Statement on Denominational Inclusiveness," p. 7, footnote.
[112] This is how Luther's Large and Small Catechisms talk about the work of God's Holy Spirit in the Apostles' Creed.
[113] Fred B. Craddock wrote a book entitled *Overhearing the Gospel* (St. Louis MO: Chalice Press, 2002) with the premise that indirect communication through a story or an example is often a very effective way of communicating the gospel.

BIBLIOGRAPHY

Books

The Book of Concord: The Confessions of the Evangelical Lutheran Church, translated and edited by Theodore G. Tappert, Philadelphia: Fortress Press, 1959.

Das, Andrew A. *Baptized Into God's Family.* Milwaukee WI: Northwestern Publishing House, 1991.

Graham, Billy. *How to Be Born Again.* New York: Warner Books, 1977.

Hobbs, Herschel H. *The Baptist Faith and Message.* Nashville TN: Convention Press, 1971.

Koester, Robert. *Law and Gospel: Foundation of Lutheran Ministry.* Milwaukee WI: Northwestern Publishing House, 1993.

Kuske, David P. *Luther's Catechism.* WELS Board for Parish Services. Milwaukee WI: Northwestern Publishing House, 1982.

Leppien, Patsy A. and J. Kincaid Smith. *What's Going On Among the Lutherans?* Milwaukee WI: Northwestern Publishing House, 1992

Luther, Martin. *What Luther Says: An Anthology.* Compiled by Ewald M. Plass, Vol. 3. St. Louis MO: Concordia Publishing House, 1959.

Mead, Frank S. *Handbook of Denominations in the United States.* Nashville TN: Abingdon Press, 1983.

Pieper, Francis. *Christian Dogmatics.* Volume 3. St. Louis MO: Concordia Publishing House, 1953.

Schuetze, Armin, and Irwin Habeck. *The Shepherd Under Christ.* Milwaukee WI: Northwestern Publishing House, 1974.

Periodicals

Brug, John. "The Lutheran Doctrine of Sanctification and Its Rivals." *Wisconsin Lutheran Quarterly.* Vol. 101, No. 3 (Summer 2004).

Siggelkow, Alan H. "Pastoral Leadership From the Perspective of Church History." *Wisconsin Lutheran Quarterly.* Vol. 101, No. 3 (Summer 2004).

Vallesky, David. "Evangelical Lutheranism and Today's Evangelicals and Fundamentalists." *Wisconsin Lutheran Quarterly.* Vol. 80, No. 3 (Summer 1983).

Internet Sources

For "The 1689 Confession of Faith": http://www.prbc.org/Confession.htm.

For the original of "The 1677/89 London Baptist Confession of Faith (BCF Assistant)": http://64.33.81.65/baptists/1689/original/1689bc.html.

For American Baptist Churches—USA: http://www.abc-usa.org.

For Savastio, "What Is a Reformed Baptist Church?": http://www.prbc.org/ReformedBaptist.htm.

For the Southern Baptist Convention: http://www.sbc.net.